BRIGHT NOTES

THE DAY OF THE LOCUST BY NATHANAEL WEST

Intelligent Education

Nashville, Tennessee

BRIGHT NOTES: The Day of the Locust
www.BrightNotes.com

No part of this publication may be used or reproduced in any manner whatsoever without written permission, except in the case of brief quotations in critical articles and reviews. For permissions, contact Influence Publishers http://www.influencepublishers.com.

ISBN: 978-1-645423-46-1 (Paperback)
ISBN: 978-1-645423-48-5 (eBook)

Published in accordance with the U.S. Copyright Office Orphan Works and Mass Digitization report of the register of copyrights, June 2015.

Originally published by Monarch Press.
2019 Edition published by Influence Publishers.

Interior design by Lapiz Digital Services. Cover Design by Thinkpen Designs.

Printed in the United States of America.

Library of Congress Cataloging-in-Publication Data forthcoming.
Names: Intelligent Education
Title: BRIGHT NOTES: The Day of the Locust
Subject: STU004000 STUDY AIDS / Book Notes

CONTENTS

1) Introduction to Nathanael West   1

2) Textual Analysis
      Genre, Convention, Tradition   23
      General Analysis and Interpretation of The Text   34
      Sectional Analysis and Interpretation of The Text   82
      The Critics   107

3) Essay Questions and Answers   112

4) Bibliography   124

INTRODUCTION TO NATHANAEL WEST

....

NOTE TO THE STUDENT

This Critical Commentary aims to enhance your appreciation of Nathanael West's classic novel, *The Day of the Locust*. It will make little sense to you unless you are already familiar with the original text. Throughout his critical discussion, Professor Chatterton assumes that his comments will prompt you to refer back to West's work. In his "Annotated Bibliography," Professor Chatterton lists current editions of *The Day of the Locust*, including paperback editions most frequently used by students

- The Editors

"THE DAY OF THE LOCUST" AND THE WESTIAN WORLD

In writing his four short novels, Nathanael West conceived and created a fictional world unique in American literature and perhaps in the literature of any other culture. It is a highly selective world - one from which large areas of the American culture are eliminated altogether, in order for particular aspects of American life to emerge from the fiction highlighted and intensified. The same is true of the characters in West's novels.

For the most part they are people created specifically for the highly selective world which West has drawn for their habitation.

And this is a world incapable of producing a "hero." It is a world sick with spiritual malaise. In West's own words it is a "half-world." But the half-world of West's novels is a distillation of social and cultural properties that make American life what it is, as opposed to what it ought to be, or even what it could be.

The importance of the Westian world lies in West's unique perception of the relationships between contemporary American life and the eternal condition of mankind. In order to understand these relationships, West was forced to look hard and deep into the external circumstances of his own life and into the recesses of his inner being. Between the two he found almost insuperable discrepancies, and out of his efforts to resolve the discrepancies came his fiction. Few other writers have striven so seriously to reconcile their inner with their outer selves. Even fewer have managed to do so without succumbing to easy rationalizations. But West saw himself and his world with stark and terrifying clarity, and the value of his fiction lies in his capacity as an artist to depict with equal clarity the irreconcilables which exist everywhere in modern man's imperfect and sometimes bizarre relationships with his universe.

In many ways, *The Day of the Locust* is West's most mature and most disturbing depiction of these irreconcilables and of their potentially destructive, even apocalyptic, power. Josephine Herbst contends that "the clue to the unique quality in the fiction of Nathanael West lies more in what he recoiled from than in what he embraced" (Nathanael West, *A Collection of Critical Essays*, p. 21). In this respect, *The Day of the Locust* offers the best insight into the unique quality of West's fiction, since it reflects the broadest spectrum of those things which the author recoiled from, including some of those which he had already explored in his three earlier novels. At any rate, one can gain a clear view of West's life and career only by seeing the biographical "facts" apart from those things which he simultaneously embraced and recoiled from - that is, by seeing the "outer man" and the "inner man" as different but component parts of the "whole man" as artist.

THE OUTER WORLD OF NATHANAEL WEST

Childhood (1903–1917)

Nathanael West was born Nathan (though it was later changed to Nathaniel before it became Nathanael) von Wallenstein Weinstein in New York City on October 17, 1903. His mother was Anna Wallenstein and his father Max Weinstein, both of them the offspring of families that had been closely related by blood and marriage for several generations. Both families were German-Jewish in origin, and both had been expelled for political reasons from the same area of Russia. Living in New York during the last decade of the nineteenth century, they considered themselves true and complete Americans, and they communicated among themselves in German and in English but not in Yiddish or in Russian. Anna was a devoted mother; Max a successful builder of large apartment-house complexes. Max was almost obsessed with the desire to provide for his children all the "good things" which America offered. He wanted desperately for his children to know at first hand something other than life in the big and confining city. Above all, he wanted them to be well educated in order to become thoroughly acceptable to at least the upper middle classes of American society. As a boy, therefore, young Nathan was sent away from the city to spend most of his summers with his mother on a farm in Connecticut. Here, as

Jay Martin has observed, the boy began to feel "something of the primitive mystery of the American land" (Nathanael West, p. 23). At this farm, and later at summer camps in the mountains, Nathan came to love the outdoors and "to regard the wilderness as powerfully curative of the city ills" (Martin, Nathanael West, p. 23). Consumed by the wish to become "instant Americans," the Weinsteins had consciously striven to erase their past altogether, and without the active sense of a cultural past, the Weinstein children found themselves adrift in the complex patterns of American life, which they were expected to assimilate completely and without question.

School And College Days (1908-1926)

In 1908, West began his public schooling at P.S. 81. This was the first public school in New York to be used for the training of teachers. It was also the earliest to adopt "progressive" methods of education to replace formal and conventional methods. In 1915, West made initial plans to attend P.S. 10, but instead he switched to P.S. 186, where he finished the eighth grade. From his first day in the public schools, his attitude toward institutionalized education was at best cavalier and his attendance highly irregular. His grades were seldom better than average. While his classmates were skipping grades - which was normal practice in those times - he remained in the grade that corresponded to his age. Even there he was usually listed among the "average" students instead of among the "brighter" members of the class. In 1917, he entered De Witt Clinton High School, but he attended so irregularly and failed so many courses that he took an extra year to achieve junior class standing. During these years he spent most of his summers at a conventionally organized summer camp maintained for middle-class Jewish children at Lake Paradox in the Adirondacks. In June 1920, he left high school without completing graduation requirements, and in the fall of 1921, under the name Nathaniel Weinstein, he entered Tufts College on the strength of a high school transcript which he had altered to record at least passing credit in the required high school courses. At Tufts he spent freely the generous allowances provided by his father. He dressed well and enjoyed a busy social life, but yielding to what had become a kind of habit, he rarely attended classes. At mid-term he had failed all his courses and was told to withdraw from the college. Since these F's were only interim marks, however, they had not been placed upon any of the Tufts records. Moreover, whether by accident or by deliberate manipulation, West came into possession of a transcript of credit belonging to another Tufts student who was also named Nathan Weinstein. On the strength of this record, West entered Brown University in the spring of 1922. Without a high school diploma and without passing grades from Tufts, but by taking advantage of pure coincidence, West made arrangements to enter Brown as a mid-year sophomore. Here, too, he dressed remarkably well in Brooks Brothers clothing. He maintained an avid interest in sports, and even more avidly he pursued the arts. Using free passes that were provided him by the drama critic of the Providence Journal, he regularly attended the legitimate theaters. He rarely missed the local showing of a motion picture. Though in the spring of 1922 the authorities at Brown suspended him for excessive absences, he was readmitted in the fall. After becoming active on the staff of the campus literary magazine, he was graduated from Brown with the degree of Ph.B. in June 1924.

Paris (1926–1927)

After marking time for a year in his father's construction business, West realized that he was rapidly losing touch with the world of arts and letters. In the fall of 1926, supported by his family, he embarked for Paris, where he hoped to be accepted as one of the young writers and artists who were known by then as the expatriates of the "lost generation." By living this life he hoped to discover whether he could, indeed, become a successful writer of fiction. Though he worked sporadically on *The Dream Life of Balso Snell*, he actually did very little sustained writing in Paris. Instead, he spent most of his time observing the Parisian life of the expatriates and of the French people themselves, and he acquired a feeling for the rapidly passing phases of Dada and for the more substantial influences of surrealism upon contemporary art and literature. After only three months in Paris, he returned home in January 1927. Though his visit had lasted only a comparatively short time, its importance to his development as a novelist was out of all proportion to its brevity.

New York (1927–1933)

Novels published during this period: *The Dream Life of Balso Snell* (spring 1931); *Miss Lonelyhearts* (April 1933). Forced to come home from Europe early in 1927 as a result of a serious decline in the family construction business, West took a convenient position as night clerk at the Kenmore Hall Hotel in New York City. Much earlier, during his two years at Brown University, West had begun working on portions and fragments of a novel that eventually became *The Dream Life of Balso Snell*. Between 1927 and 1929 he wrote and rewrote *Balso Snell* over and over again, and it was not published until 1931. In March of 1929, after reading a batch of real "advice to the lovelorn" letters which a columnist known as "Susan Chester" had offered to S. J. Perelman, West began writing *Miss Lonelyhearts*. In the fall of 1930, he became manager of the Sutton Club Hotel, where he worked for about a year and where he provided a free hostelry for other struggling writers, including James T. Farrell and Dashiell Hammett. In 1931 he took a leave from the Sutton in order to work full time on his writing at a rented cabin in the Adirondacks. After several months of writing here and in a Bucks County farmhouse which he owned jointly with the Perelmans, West returned briefly to New York. There he continued working at the Warford House in Frenchtown during October and November of 1932. For a short time in 1932 he served with William Carlos Williams as an editor of Contact, and then, having completed *Miss Lonelyhearts*, he returned to his job at the Sutton Hotel. *Miss Lonelyhearts* was accepted and put into print by Liveright in 1933. From advance copies the novel received good reviews, but before the first printing was released the publishing firm went bankrupt. Months later, with the whole first printing bought up and released by another publisher, the earlier reviews had lost their impact upon the reading public. Of the first printing, only about 800 copies were sold, mostly at reduced rates. From the combined sales of *The Dream Life of Balso Snell*, *Miss Lonelyhearts*, and *A Cool Million West* was to receive only about $780.

Hollywood (1933–1940)

Novels published during this period: *A Cool Million* (June 1934); *The Day of the Locust* (May 1939). During the summer of 1933, West was in Hollywood working as a junior writer for Columbia pictures. While the movie version of *Miss Lonelyhearts* was being made by Darryl F. Zanuck at *Twentieth Century Fox*, West prepared conventional movie "treatments" for popular farces and light comedies, none of which reached production. At about the time when the badly mutilated version of *Miss Lonelyhearts* was released, West's Columbia contract ended, and he went back to the East for a time before he returned to Hollywood in the spring of 1935. Previously, in the fall of 1933, during his stay on the Bucks County farm, West had begun work on *A Cool Million*, and it had been published in June 1934. Though its rights were sold to *Columbia Pictures*, the story was never filmed, and reviews of the book were so lukewarm that within a year the edition was remaindered at twenty-five cents a copy. To West's further disappointment, he failed to get a Guggenheim fellowship upon which he had placed his hopes for assistance. Desperately in need of money, and intrigued by the idea of using Hollywood and life in moviedom as the subject of a novel, he returned to Hollywood in the late spring of 1935. For several months during this trying time he was unable to find work with any of the studios. But in January 1936 he managed to get a temporary contract as a script writer for *Republic Productions*. After four months here at a weekly salary of $200 a week, he signed a six months contract for $250 a week. Thereafter, while reaming out movie adaptations and continuities for *Republic* and other motion picture studios, he spent his spare time working on the manuscript of *The Day of the Locust*. In May 1938, under the title of *The Cheated*, his last novel was accepted for publication by Random House. While awaiting the appearance of his novel, he left his most recent job with *RKO* and went back to New York to collaborate with Joseph Schrank on a legitimate stage play, Good Hunting, which for a number of outre and unpredictable reasons closed after only two performances in November 1938. Absolutely broke, but with promises of a job at *Universal*, West drove back to Hollywood, where he anxiously wore out the weeks in waiting for the imminent publication of his "Hollywood novel." On the proofs he altered the title from The Cheated to its permanent phrasing, *The Day of the Locust*, and the novel appeared on the bookstore shelves in May 1938. Though it received a considerable number of highly favorable reviews, it sold fewer than 1,500 copies and was, of course, a financial failure. Planning yet another novel, and desultorily making notes for it, West continued as a script writer for *Universal* and *RKO*, for whom he created some scripts that eventually became successful motion pictures. As usual, he appears to have been hoping to make enough money at script writing to support him while he finished the manuscript for his current novel. But in April the ordinary routines of his life and career were subordinated to his marriage to Eileen McKenney. After two or three months of delayed vacation in Oregon, they returned to Hollywood, where West became more and more successful as a script writer for the studios. On December 22, 1940, coming home with his wife from a hunting trip in Mexico, West did not see a stop sign and collided with another car. Both he and Eileen were killed almost instantly.

THE INNER TERRAIN OF NATHANAEL WEST

Heritage Without Myth (1903–1917)

To the little boy who was named Nathan Weinstein - but who would also call himself Nathaniel von Wallenstein Weinstein and later Nathanael West - the childhood years in and near New York City were times of religious and cultural confusion. During these formative years, West was caught in the extraordinarily rapid and wholesale transition of his family from their Russian - Jewish origins, which they wished to abandon entirely, to the established traditions of American urban life, all of which the family tried to absorb at once. In Russia, both the Weinsteins and the Wallensteins had preferred to live as Germans rather than as Jews or even as Russians. In America, they tried to obliterate everything Russian and Jewish in their past, in order to become thoroughly and almost instantly American.

Young Nathan seemed expected to pretend that the Russian generations on both sides of his family had been neither Russian nor Jewish but primarily German. Even their German heritage was to be minimized in order that the family could adopt uncluttered the attitudes and the folkways of the "commercial" or "work-ethic" society in America. Deprived of a cultural past, young Nathan was confronted with the necessity to absorb American values and habits of thought and behavior instantaneously and almost indiscriminately.

But unlike his father, who was eager to adopt unquestioningly everything American - names, dress, manners, customs, economics - the little boy was incapable of accepting among his own personal attributes anything that he could not test against some meaningful scale of values. In this important respect the inner world of Nathanael West came very early into direct conflict with his outer world, as represented by his family, his religion, and the society in which he was expected to find his way. As one critic has said, West "was prototypically a marginal man, perched uneasily on the edge of his society" (Jonathan Raban, "A Surfeit of Commodities," p. 218). And in his review of Martin's biography of West (Nation, August 17, 1970), Richard Giannone observes that in the aloneness and divisiveness of a life outside a traditional context, "West tried to make himself new out of his own weaknesses. He made of his division an artistic wholeness; of his alienation a moral perspective."

To a considerable extent, the first fourteen years of West's life represent a long period of search for selfhood inside a family that was alienated from its Russian-Jewish origins. Equally, it was a period in West's life when he had to prepare himself to be treated as a Jew in a world from which he had consciously and deliberately eliminated whatever might have remained of his "Jewishness." As matters turned out, he struggled with this problem to the end of his days. He was never entirely free from this struggle, especially in his own mind.

The Nostrums Of Normalcy (1908-1924)

By the time West enrolled in his first public school he had already developed a marked aversion to all forms of conventional and institutional authority. Brought up to ignore everything Russian and Jewish in his family background and to create a cultural context for himself day by day, West feared that he was in danger of becoming an American without a distinctive selfhood, without an identity. Quick and encyclopedic of mind, active and fertile of imagination, independent and self-reliant by temperament, he managed to create a considerable part of his own private world by a sustained application of his powers of fancy and fantasy. In this realm he created identities for himself, of which some were impossible of fulfillment in the actual world. Others, however, became part of West's everyday vision of himself. Later in his life, for instance, he was in a measure able to fulfill his early vision of himself as hunter and pathfinder. But such things as his horrendous account of a trip down the Salmon River of the Northwest remained part of a purely fanciful repertoire - wishes fulfilled only in the imagination.

In the active life of his fancy, West freely indulged his fascination with everything bizarre and grotesque, just as in his everyday life he preferred the bizarre and the grotesque to the mundane. For the same reasons he asserted and often over-asserted his individuality by rejecting everything traditional and orthodox in his family life, in his schooling, in business, in art, and in society. Except under the utmost financial duress he refused the entreaties of his family to work in their construction business or to adopt any of the "responsible" or "creditable" professions which they urged him to enter. From his earliest school days he refused to attend classes, whatever other school activities he might pursue upon his own terms. Though he was a wide and voracious reader throughout all his school and college years, he refused to accept the formal structure of class assignments, and he rebelled against all attempts to evaluate his attainments by means of standard testing programs. In one way or another, West sought to establish and maintain his own identity by rebelling against almost every major institution that was part of the society into which he had been born.

During his public school and college years, West began to see that, like every other young American of his generation, he was in danger of becoming the docile servant of **conventions** and institutions. Even in his earliest years in the public schools, West rebelled against the tyranny of fads and fashions. Indeed, he not only opposed conventional values but sought to distinguish himself by pursuing their opposites. He took perverse pride, therefore, in failing the required public school courses and in achieving an eminently bad record of attendance while he assiduously applied himself to the attendance of all the stage plays in the theaters along 125th Street. Instead of applying himself to the courses of study devised by the teachers and the administrators of the city school system, he haunted museums and used-book stores.

During his public school years he developed a pattern of behavior that he followed with variations and embellishments all the way through his hectic and erratic college career. In Providence, Rhode Island, while he was a student at Brown University, he lived by the behavioral patterns which he had already established for his own peculiar life-and mind-style, but by now he had discovered interesting embellishments. For the legitimate theaters he had free tickets supplied by a friend and drama critic, and when there was no new stage play he could attend the movies, which were in their infancy but available in big cities.

Moreover, his methods of revolt became more subtle and refined. In some ways, he found, as he also found later in writing his novels, that he could more effectively oppose social **conventions** by means of **parody**. During his college years he insisted upon dressing meticulously in the Brooks Brothers fashions of the era. In both manner and costume he appears to have been trying to live a **parody** of these fashions, just as he sometimes did with his interest in most of the common diversions of the age, including organized sports. From West's interest in sports may have come his feeling that "getting ahead" in an institutionalized society depends largely upon how well one "plays the game, " and the ingenuity with which he "played the game" of getting a college degree suggests that he was living a **parody** of this elaborate game by egregiously overplaying it. The same assumption helps to explain also why West did not hesitate to use any ploy necessary to achieve his college degree.

Dada And Surrealism (1924–1926)

Dada was an intense but short-lived movement that began during World War I and flourished during the period immediately following the war. The word Dada itself was intended to be meaningless, much as "baby talk" is meaningless, and the term was applied to a loose-knit, almost formless group of artists and writers who believed that there was no meaning in anything in their world. Therefore they revolted against all rules and regulations, all forms of **convention**, all traditional procedures. To the Dadaist, everything in life was pointless, including art and literature. Therefore the Dadaists devoted themselves to creating art and literature that was deliberately pointless and meaningless. Philosophically, Dada was a nihilist movement.

When West was in Paris in 1926, many of the expatriates had been Dadaists, and the effects of that movement were still quite strong among the young artists and writers, even though Dada had merged with, and had largely lost itself in, a much more substantial and constructive movement called Surrealism. In France, where this movement first began in the years following World War I, Surrealism grew out of Dada, and it shares with Dada a distrust of all traditional standards, especially in literature and art. As an important constructive factor, however, Surrealism applies the basic principles of Freudian psychoanalysis to the creative processes of literature and of art in general. The Surrealist knows that man's deepest impulses are buried in the complex life of the subconscious and the preconscious, whence they must be drawn out, much as they emerge in dreams and hallucinations - disordered, disproportionate, bizarre, defiant of reason and logic.

During his three months' sojourn among the literary exiles in Paris in the fall of 1926, West was liberally exposed to Dada, and he was strongly attracted to the movement, even though it was in its protracted death-throes. In the basic beliefs of Dadaism West saw, as Malcolm Cowley would later see (*Exiles Return*, p. 149), that "Dada in art and life was the extreme of individualism."

In the burgeoning "school" of Surrealism, too, West was vitally interested. He was attracted to the Surrealist idea that dreams and even fantasies are the source of truth in me world, and he was willing to believe that this perception is the key to the universal chaos which characterizes life in the twentieth century. Moreover, his macabre sense of humor was particularly congenial to the Surrealist notion that all conventional human relationships are empty and meaningless, the product of a rational world that must give way to individual perceptions.

To both Dada and Surrealism, then, West's novels owe a good deal.

During his last two years at Brown, West had been brightly aware of the Dadaist "happenings" and the Dadaist literary experiments that were sweeping across Europe. He was fascinated by reports that Dada readings were being held in public rest rooms, and he sympathized mildly with the Dada declarations of artistic freedom. As he endlessly worked and reworked the early drafts of *The Dream Life of Balso Snell*, he created a few typical Dada "stunts" of his own, for the delectation of his classmates. He once combined two Dadaist poems to form a single Dada poem, for example. By the time he had left college and had worked for nearly a year upon his father's construction projects, however, most of the widespread Dada agitation had gradually subsided in Europe, and West began to feel that he was missing all the most important literary fermentations of a crucial era in the development of twentieth-century literature and art. For the first time he realized that he must either accept the family's construction business as his life work, or make an all-out effort to establish himself as a writer. Choosing to make himself look like a writer by going where a large number of young writers had gone in order to learn from each other, West behaved according to the current nostrum that "in order to be an artist, one has to live like one."

In Paris, however, West refused to live according to the images which the expatriate artists and writers had created for themselves. Instead of "starving in a garret," he lived quite affluently. As he had done at college, he dressed smartly, and instead of laboring conscientiously on *The Dream Life of Balso Snell*, West spent most of his time in conversation at the various bars and cafes that were the hangouts for artists in exile. After about three months he had to go back home to help salvage the family's foundering construction enterprises, and he brought with him very little of a concrete nature - not even a finished manuscript - to show for his expensive sojourn among the literary exiles who were rapidly becoming famous in America.

But he had accomplished some of the intangible things that were to prove invaluable to him throughout his career as a writer. He had not only seen the decline of Dada and the advent of Surrealism (to which the very title of his first novel, *The Dream Life of Balso Snell*, is ample testimony), but he had thoroughly familiarized himself with the prevailing temper of the times in which he was to live and work.

Boniface As Artist (1927-1933)

In January 1927, West came back to New York from Paris and - as it turned out - back from his last opportunity to create an identity for himself by means of wholesale rebellion. With the loss of support from the heretofore infallible family business, West was for the first time in his life cast out upon his own to meet the world at least halfway. For the first time he had to live with worldly attitudes that had been consistently objects of his scorn. Somehow he would have to compromise with business and commerce, and he would have to start thinking of writing novels for profit.

In some ways, West proved himself capable of making a remarkably complete and practical adjustment. Recognizing if not condoning the necessity for a young artist to take some form of "gainful employment" in order to survive as an artist in America, West managed to achieve within his own complex temperament a split between the practical and the artistic. Unlike many other young and struggling writers of his generation, he actually seemed able to compartmentalize his personality, consigning one part of himself to the necessary job of making a living as a hotel manager, but leaving another part of himself - the artistic side of his temperament - largely untouched and uncontaminated by his responsibilities as businessman.

Indeed, West must have perceived that, if a young novelist had to devote himself to a full-time job in the world of business, a job as hotel night-manager at the Kenmore Hall and later at the Sutton Club could offer some rather obvious advantages. Especially for a man of West's complicated personality, the night-desk job in a hotel offered limitless opportunities for observing all kinds of people and for studying their behavior under a wide variety of circumstances. While he was working at these hotels West confined his native and comprehensive rebelliousness to his relationships with close friends, who were the only persons to see this side of his character during these years. Otherwise he harbored this side of himself inside the intricacies of his active fantasy, which in turn was to feed his fiction.

In his relationships with the guests of the hotel he exercised a sense of diplomacy that surprised his many friends, to whom he seemed by turns anti-sentimental and toughly intellectual, deeply pessimistic, and frequently "touchy" about sham, pretense, and anything intellectually sterile or boring. If he managed a hotel and its many problems efficiently and well, in his unguarded moments he was nonetheless a man of startling contradictions.

For West, one advantage of his job as night manager of a hotel was the long stretch of free time that came between the last registrant at night and the wake-up calls in the early morning. Every night during this quiet time, West mulled over the stories that crowded his mind. Sometimes he actually worked on these stories, and in 1929 he published at least one short story in the magazines. He was still fascinated with Dadaism, however, and in these short occasional writings he seemed unable to resist the deliberate perpetration of literary hoaxes. In one instance he tried to fool the editors of transition into accepting a free-verse rendition of some lines which West had taken directly from Flaubert, but the editors declined to publish it. In another instance, however, he was successful in publishing in the *Overland Monthly* a mock-Western tall tale written in the manner of Bret Harte and Mark Twain. Even though these entertaining hoaxes are excellent evidence of West's extraordinary talent for creating trenchant **parody**, West decided by 1930 that his talents were not best suited for the short story.

At this time, then, West began devoting himself seriously and almost exclusively to the short, close-knit novel in the French tradition, which he knew well and greatly admired. Under this impulse he managed to finish *The Dream Life of Balso Snell*, after several years of desultory labor and almost countless revisions. While Balso Snell was being turned down by one publisher after another, West went immediately to work on *Miss Lonelyhearts*. By the time *Balso Snell* was published as a Contact Edition in 1931, West was already well along with the composition of *Miss Lonelyhearts*, and he had come to grips with the necessity for "gainful employment" on the one hand and the artist's need for periods of undisturbed productivity on the other. From this time on, he regarded his regular jobs as ways of getting money enough to live on while he finished his novels. Whenever he had managed to save enough money as boniface at the Kenmore or the Sutton, he took a leave in order to devote himself to his writing in some remote place like his Bucks County farmhouse. In this fashion he completed the writing of *Miss Lonelyhearts*, published in 1933. From 1927 to the end of his life, however, West managed to live simultaneously in the world of ordinary commerce and in the writer's world of creative imagination, and to do so without allowing either of these disparate worlds to impede the necessary functions of the other.

Craft Versus Art (1933–1940)

In the summer of 1933, while waiting for the filming of *Miss Lonelyhearts*, West found he could make a substantial living as a script writer for the Hollywood studios. From this time on, though Hollywood employment proved much more erratic and unreliable than his various positions as hotel manager, he preferred to live in Hollywood and to work as a script writer while he planned and wrote his novels. In this regard he was influenced by the fact that large numbers of his New York friends and acquaintances were already in Hollywood doing the same thing. His close friend and brother-in-law S. J. Perelman was writing successful scripts for the Marx Brothers movies, and even so unlikely a writer as the shy Erskine Caldwell had joined the stampede of successful writers to the city which gossip columnists were christening "Tinseltown."

In the commercial sense, however, West was not a "successful" author. Therefore, while his friends openly scoffed at Hollywood for its air of insanity, its crass commercialism, and its total indifference to real art, West remained altogether dependent upon his Hollywood script assignments for financial support while he wrote his novels. Indeed, when he failed to get a Guggenheim grant in 1934 he began to realize that script writing was his only source of income. In order to get enough money to live upon while he wrote his novels, he would have to reconcile himself to doing regular "hack work" for the film industry.

In some ways West's emotional and intellectual adjustment to the "Hollywood scene" was even more remarkable than his earlier reconciliation to the world of business in New York. Except for a few brief sojourns in New York and elsewhere, West lived in Hollywood from 1933 to the end of his life, and during this considerable period of time he managed somehow to perform regular "hack writing" for the movie studios without allowing this activity to diminish the artistic values of his fiction. To his mind, the writing of a movie script was essentially a craft that demanded of him an elemental competence, but nothing more. He carefully avoided thinking of his script writing as any form or variety of art, and in these pursuits he steadfastly refused to give of himself more than mere script-crafting demanded.

It is a monument to the "tough intellectualism" in his character that they could keep the two kinds of literary composition entirely separate in his mind, as though the one had nothing at all to do with the other. During his long hours at the studio he could work rapidly upon a movie script, composing off the top of his head as it were, pouring out page after page of easy dialogue by way of dictation to a secretary, and seldom correcting or revising. Then he could go home to work upon the manuscript of *A Cool Million* or *The Day of the Locust*, whose pages he would compose painfully, rewriting and polishing laboriously, taking infinite care with every phrase, every image, every passage, never quite satisfied that he had achieved the perfection he demanded of himself.

Moreover, he found Hollywood and its peculiar denizens endlessly fascinating. From his first few days in the great American capital of big money and infinite dreams, he was consciously preparing himself to capture the essence of the place in his fiction, and he did so at last in *The Day of the Locust*. From the first he had seen clearly that to the huge mass of middle-class Americans - to the horde of "common people" - Hollywood seemed a siren-land of dreams, beckoning with all the promises that the ordinary American had ever hoped to see fulfilled within himself. But he saw just as clearly that Hollywood left all such dreams empty and abandoned in vast "dream-dumps" on the forlorn back lots of the studios. Here, then, to Hollywood, came all those who wished to act out the American dream in a shadow-life of celluloid, and here too came those untold thousands of mere "watchers" or "starers" for whom the dream-makers manufactured their dreams. To these people, both actors and starers, all of whom are imperceptibly being cheated of the dreams for which they have learned to live, a day of apocalyptic violence is not far distant. These are the people of whom West writes in *The Day of the Locust*, and the ending of the novel depicts their apocalyptic surge of violence and comprehensive destruction.

Nathanael West: The Synthesis of His Art

Because West could never entirely reconcile the warring elements of his inner and his outer worlds, he remained throughout his life a precariously integrated personality. But in his fiction he was able to synthesize many of the disparate elements that he could not reconcile within himself. If indeed he was a marginal man, divided partly against himself and partly against the society in which he had to live, he was nonetheless an artist who could make of his own weaknesses the main strength of his art. In his novels he made of his alienation an integrated whole, an aesthetic world in which, as artist, he could belong. In his art he created a new self, and, in the words of Richard Giannone ("Freaks, Con Men, Hustlers," p. 122), "that new self could live in art which became the patria he did not find elsewhere."

Within the older traditions of the comic narrative West created for himself his own tradition, compounded of forms and structures that seemed new in their unique combinations of stark, startling, and often violent imagery. These combinations have become West's own "style," in the most comprehensive sense of that term (that is, in the recent sense that "style" is "all the choices that a writer makes in the process of composition"). West's "style" is recognizable anywhere. It is unmistakably Nathanael West's, and no other. This "style" is the synthesis of West's otherwise divided and alienated selfhood.

THE DAY OF THE LOCUST

TEXTUAL ANALYSIS

GENRE, CONVENTION, TRADITION

"THE DAY OF THE LOCUST" AS A "SHORT NOVEL"

By every meaningful measure, all four of West's principal works are "novellas" or short novels. Even though in the gross measure represented by mere word-count *The Day of the Locust* is considerably longer than the three earlier novels of West, that novel, like the others, falls unquestionably into the domain of the short novel, which is generally supposed to be not shorter than 15,000 nor longer than 50,000 words. Therefore *The Day of the Locust* must be analyzed and interpreted as a contribution to the special literary form which has come to be called the short novel.

In selecting the short novel as the principal medium of his art, West defends his choice by drawing a straight line of influence from the literary criticism of Edgar Allan Poe to the mass temperament of mid-twentieth-century American readers. Despite the widely held critical consensus which proclaims Poe the "father of the short story," Nathanael West is probably the only important writer of twentieth-century American fiction who has publicly acknowledged his direct indebtedness to Poe's remarks upon the interdependence of "effect" and "extent." Briefly outlined, the burden of Poe's "The Philosophy of Composition" (1846)is that the writer of imaginative literature must strive foremost to achieve a "unity of impression" which he cannot hope to maintain if the "literary work" is too long to be read at "one sitting," since in the interval between sittings "the affairs of the world interfere, and everything like totality is at once destroyed." Insisting upon the provision that "a certain degree of duration is absolutely requisite for the production of any effect at all," Poe nonetheless argues convincingly that there is no advantage in a long work that can be said to "counterbalance the loss of unity which attends it." Moreover, says Poe, "all intense excitements are, through a psychal necessity, brief." Therefore it is of the utmost importance that the writer of imaginative literature recognize the existence of an almost mathematical principle which requires that the brevity of the literary work "must be in direct ratio to the intensity of the intended effect."

To West - who thoroughly understood and appreciated this principle of "psychal necessity" - Poe's arguments for controlled brevity suggested a solution to the twentieth-century reader's demand for a literary mode that is compatible with the fast pace and the crowded lives of contemporary Americans. "Forget the **epic**, the master work," West writes in "Some Notes on Miss L." "In America," he continues, "fortunes do not accumulate, the soil does not grow, families have no history...you have only time to explode."

Yet the literary form into which West has chosen to explode is not so much the short story - in which he experiments only infrequently and not nearly so successfully - but the "novella." To West, it appears, Poe's demand for "a certain degree of duration" is better answered by the "novella" than by the briefer explosion of the short story, and certainly better than by the briefest of all such explosions, the short short story. Conversely, the tradition of the leisurely or the discursive or the encyclopedic novel strikes West as altogether inappropriate to contemporary American readers. As West sees them, in their daily lives these readers are "a hasty people," and they are therefore much too forgiving of novelists like Pearl Buck, Theodore Dreiser, and Sinclair Lewis - that is, too forgiving of those authors who in theory and practice are obvious advocates of the "big novel."

In America, however, many of our best authors have persevered in the writing of highly significant short novels without ever establishing anything that can legitimately be called a "tradition" of the short novel. In a culture where the **conventions** of the "big novel" and the "short story" are reasonably clear and mutually discriminating, the fictional tale of intermediate dimensions has always appeared somehow indeterminate. Yet in the literature of the Western world the history of the "novella" goes back at least as far as Boccaccio, and in our own time Henry James has bestowed upon it his special sanction as a "blessed" form. For Nathanael West, the short novel was the fictional mode best suited to his need to "explode" into literary creation, and at the same time it appears to have given him the best vehicle to offer a fast-paced, fragmented American society. These were the "hasty people" into whose keeping West stood ready to relinquish his fiction.

Though American readers have never altogether overcome a habitual tendency to speak of the short novel and the short story as jointly comprising a category of literature which they designate "short fiction," the practice of the best writers has been to construct the short novel according to the basic architectural principles of the novel proper. Structurally, then, the short novel is a novel rather than some variety of short story, and this distinction remains an essential one in any discussion of the "novella." The main difference lies in the comparative complexity of structure, and if this basis of distinction between the short story and the short novel can be considered a legitimate basis, William Wasserstrom's definition of the short novel is one of the clearest and most useful of all recent attempts to create a working definition of the "novella."

In his introduction to *The Modern Short Novel* (New York, 1965), Wasserstrom contends that "the short novel is equipped with a complex plot, each incident of which is calculated to expose the self, in all its vulnerability and solitariness, to one particular but representative process whereby the world manifests its will to dominion over individual men." Obviously this statement is intended as a "working" definition rather than as a formulation of some theoretical "law" which the critic hopes to advance as some inviolable principle that must be observed by all who attempt the literary form. On the contrary, it is a diagnostic definition, derived from close and comprehensive analysis of short novels that are already part of our literary heritage. As a "descriptive definition" it is sufficiently clear and concrete to suggest to the student the distinctive character of the short novel and to provide a workable basis for analyzing and interpreting *The Day of the Locust.*

"THE DAY OF THE LOCUST" AS A "HOLLYWOOD NOVEL"

The Day of the Locust belongs to a special category of American novels that have become known as "Hollywood novels." In American literature this phenomenon is a comparatively recent development. Indeed, the "Hollywood novel" came into being during the early years of the Hollywood film industry, fifty or sixty years ago. Since that time at least five hundred of these novels have been published in the United States alone.

By an informal consensus among critics and scholars, *The Day of the Locust* may be considered the best example of this recent but prolific variety of American novel. Of all the authors who have written novels that are wholly or partly about Hollywood and the motion picture industry, Nathanael West has most successfully depicted the falsity and the emptiness of the Hollywood "scene" as an inescapable product of the "Great American Dream." In *The Day of the Locust*, the entire Hollywood cosmos functions as a complex symbol of the dream world, the special world of illusion which twentieth-century Americans have created for themselves. Of all the Hollywood novels, moreover, *The Day of the Locust* has demonstrated most forcibly the sheer horror of the unreality and the emptiness in the lives of those people to whom the "Hollywood Dream" is essentially the "American Dream" - a reflection and a distortion of it, perhaps, but nonetheless the "American Dream" which the average American pursues under the illusion that it offers him "the good life."

Among the earliest writers of Hollywood novels there were opposing views of the quality of life in the film capital. In *The Old Nest* (1922), for instance, Rupert Hughes provided a favorable picture of movie-making as a means of livelihood. But in the same year Harry Leon Wilson's *Merton of the Movies* satirized the make-believe world that was being offered the public by stereotyped and silly motion pictures. Even more it ridiculed the immature people who took that world seriously. Subsequently the Hollywood novel tended more and more to satirize Hollywood life, and the **satire** became more and more bitter.

In the 1930s, besides *The Day of the Locust*, there were several attempts to depict Hollywood as the American Dream turned nightmare. In his unfinished novel *The Last Tycoon*, F. Scott Fitzgerald showed the gradual disintegration of one of the legendary movie-makers whose almost dictatorial powers as production wizard and business magnate had seemed unassailable forever. In Horace McCoy's two popular novels *They Shoot Horses, Don't They?* (1935) and *I Should Have Stayed Home* (1938), the author showed how people of limited intelligence and no talent are destroyed by the cruelty and the inhumanity of the movie capital. Of the several hundred Hollywood novels that have been published to the present time, however, only *The Last Tycoon* and *The Day of the Locust* have achieved any real stature in the history of American letters. The Last Tycoon cannot be judged fairly, of course, because it was left unfinished.

"THE DAY OF THE LOCUST" AS A "COMIC NOVEL"

The exact nature of West's fiction has evaded clear and simple definition. Consequently, many critics and reviewers have misunderstood the dominant tone and quality of his work. In 1939, following publication of *The Day of the Locust*, West was tired of being criticized on grounds that seemed irrelevant to his work. Embittered by the commercial failure of *The Day of the Locust*, he wrote a letter to George Milburn, remarking that his own novels "always fall between the different schools of writing. The radical press, although I consider myself on their side, doesn't like my particular kind of joking,...and the literature boys, whom I detest, detest me in turn." In the apt phrase "my particular kind of joking," West defined for his critics and his readers the essential quality of his work. His fiction is founded upon a unique and special kind of "joking." The essence of his work is a highly individual comic sense upon which everything in his storytelling depends for its ultimate effect.

As West's remark indicates, however, many of his readers and many of his critics do not like this kind of "joking," and it seems probable that if his reviewers have not understood his peculiar sense of the comic, West himself has been sometimes unsure of its precise nature and its comic potential as a storytelling medium. There is no doubt, however, that he considered his novels essentially comic. As he once declared in a letter to Malcolm Cowley, "I'm a comic writer and it seems impossible for me to handle any of the 'big things' without seeming to laugh or at least smile."

As West made clear at one point in the book plan which he submitted for his unsuccessful Guggenheim application, he saw in the contemporary world a necessity to laugh at everything, including such large and essentially serious matters as love and death. By temperament he seems to have been impressed almost equally by the ludicrous and the horrible, and he was strongly inclined to perceive the whole world as a phenomenon that is balanced precariously upon some thin dividing line between the comic and the horrific. At any rate, in a letter to F. Scott Fitzgerald, West admitted that the reactions of readers and critics had eventually forced him to acknowledge that he was always driven by a compulsion to "go on making what one critic called 'private and unfunny jokes.'"

This compulsion appears to have been an outgrowth of West's elemental view of the human condition. He could not write about human beings at all, it seems, without resorting to his special brand of comedy as a way of masking the otherwise intolerable absurdity of the human spectacle. To West, this spectacle could be honestly and accurately depicted only in terms of the bizarre or the grotesque, and this is an attitude which Kenneth Burke has defined as "the cult of incongruity without laughter." In *The Day of the Locust*, for example, one of West's most outrageous grotesqueries is the life-sized rubber horse that lies on the bottom of Claude Estee's swimming pool. Yet in many ways the horse is no more grotesque than the general run of Hollywood people to whom West refers as "masqueraders" - those denizens of the film-town dream-factories whose houses, clothing, habits, hopes, and lives in general are all, in the words of Kingsley Widmer, "rubber imitation bad jokes" ("The Last Masquerade," p. 179).

Anything that can properly be termed "a cult of incongruity without laughter," however, must pose the question whether this kind of literary material is truly "comic" at all. But Nathanael West appears to be one of the leading innovators of a "comic" form of fiction that, if it is not "comic" in any other recent sense, is nonetheless a variety of "comedy" which found wide acceptance in American literature during the midnineteen-fifties and after. Because it has seemed to the writers of this kind of comedy that contemporary man lacks the stature and dignity appropriate to legitimate forms of tragedy, popular fiction has had to depict modern man and his life in terms of something that can be called "comic pathos." As Norman Podhoretz points out ("A Particular Kind of Joking," p. 160) this attitude is peculiarly Westian, and because West "responds to the pathos of their [most people's predicament - none of this compromises the comedy."

By the mid-sixties, therefore, when the work of Nelson Algren, Joseph Heller, and Ken Kesey began to engender a newer term - "the comic apocalyptic novel" - West was readily recognized as a pioneer, as a trailblazer and a pathfinder for those who were "discovering" the form fifteen or twenty years later. Or, if the line of these humorists can be thought to begin at least thirty years earlier with James Branch Cabell's *Jurgen*, Nathanael West is nonetheless an indispensable bridge, indeed perhaps the only bridge, between this special comic manifestation of Cabell's work in the nineteen-twenties and the savage comedy of Nelson Algren's inside-out, upside-down world of *A Walk on the Wild Side* in 1956. Both Heller's and Kesey's principal contributions to the form appeared in the early nineteen-sixties. Because the general technique of this kind of novel is to begin with the ludicrous and to move steadily toward greater and greater degrees of horror, this kind of literary work became known as "the novel of the ludicrous catastrophe," and in fiction at large the prevailing attitude gained wide currency as "black humor." During the sixties and seventies, indeed, "black humor" became the term by which all varieties of "comic pathos" were most widely identified.

Whichever of these several terms might be most appropriately applied to this peculiarly mid-twentieth-century phenomenon in American fiction, however, Nathanael West is now universally acknowledged as one of the principal early practitioners of the form - as a prime motivator of all who have followed and who will follow in this special literary **genre**. Moreover, though all four of West's novels qualify as significant contributions to the **genre**, *The Day of the Locust* seems to be recognized as its fullest expression in the Westian canon.

With regard to Nathanael West's place in the American comic tradition, however, it is important to add this short commentary: that in a culture with so short a social history as ours - that is, in a culture whose roots are still young compared with the ancient sources of the English and Continental cultures - the comic sense in our literature is still in its adolescence. In its artistic forms, the comic sense of any culture is always the direct outgrowth of the temperament and the elemental disposition of the people, and in America the comic sense has always been an ineluctable concomitant of the American self-image of the eternal adolescent. For this reason there has not been in American literature any marked tendency to develop the traditions of "high comedy" which in older cultures have been the product of their cultural maturity. In fostering and in priding themselves upon their free, ready, and open laughter, Americans have deliberately hindered the development of an ironic vision of themselves, a vision which has been for older cultures a mark of sanity and a bulwark against mistaken views of the individual person's own importance in the universal scheme of things.

For the most part, then, Americans are uncomfortable with a literature of true **satire** or hard **irony**, especially if that literature is intended as a view of their own position in a life and society which they prefer to laugh at in terms of standard banalities and conventional wheezes. The "average" American reader is not prepared to see himself as a potential loser in the universal game-plan, as one who must reconcile his own self-view with contrary realities, and as one who can do so through a strongly ironic comedy of appearance-versus-reality, as West does in *The Day of the Locust* and other novels. Another powerful American ironist, Vardis Fisher, saw clearly that "As a nation we are not ironic, and in consequence there is among us...an enormous difference between what we are and what we pretend to be" ("How's Your Sense of Humor?" p. 29). Yet, to Nathanael West, this very distance between what we are and what we pretend to be is the principal source of high comedy in the American culture. To West the horror and the anguish of the human condition is best expressed in a sharp-set form of high comedy, wherein he makes agonizingly clear just how misleading is our comfortable adolescent view of what we think we are (like the view of the people in *The Day of the Locust*, who have come to California looking for the fulfillment of their adolescent dreams), despite the evidence of all the realities that are arrayed against our habitual thoughtless laughter.

The "high comedy" of *The Day of the Locust*, then, is not in the "good old American" tradition of the early and middle career of Mark Twain, though it has some kinship with the "disillusioned" comedy of Twain's later years - "The Man That Corrupted Hadleyburg," for instance, or "The Mysterious Stranger." Westian comedy has little in common with the well-loved American comedy of "cracker-barrel sages" and "frontier yarnspinners" and "tall-tale tellers" and such American comic institutions as the "funny fat man" tradition established in the twenties and the thirties by Irvin S. Cobb. In Westian comedy there is little of the brittle and facile word play of the "Algonquin Wits" or the "slick" humor of the "New Yorker" school. But there is a close alliance between the "high comedy" of Nathanael West and the classic satirists of all ages, between the cruel comedy of West and the biting ironies of George Meredith, between the bitter humor of West and the fantastic ironies of Cabell, between the savage comedy of *The Day of the Locust* and the cosmic joking of Vardis Fisher. And if Fisher is justified in saying, "All genuine humor is ironic" ("How's Your Sense of Humor?" p. 27), *The Day of the Locust* is genuine comedy.

THE DAY OF THE LOCUST

TEXTUAL ANALYSIS

GENERAL ANALYSIS AND INTERPRETATION OF THE TEXT

CAPSULE SUMMARY OF THE PLOT

The novel depicts the failure of one popular conception of the "American Dream." The main character is Tod Hackett, a movie-set designer whose projected painting, a masterpiece called "The Burning of Los Angeles," will portray the revolt of all people cheated by the "Hollywood Dream." Homer Simpson, a shy and self-conscious hotel clerk from Iowa, is one of this horde of midwesterners who have "come to California to die." All the characters except Homer are movie industry "fringe people" - grotesques like Faye's father, Harry, a superannuated vaudeville comedian who cannot distinguish his vaudeville personalities from his real identity, and whose bizarre funeral is one of the crucial scenes. Others are the protean screenwriter Claude Estee, living in the fictional world of his scripts; the pugnacious dwarf Abe Kusich, pimp and race-track tout; and a talentless cowboy actor, Earle Shoop, who takes Faye and Tod to a vicious cockfight that remains a most memorable scene in the novel.

Both Tod and Homer are hopelessly infatuated with Faye Greener, the ultimate sex-symbol, whom Homer shelters platonically. Finding that Faye shares with a Mexican acquaintance the elemental passion which he cannot give, Homer succumbs to the long-suppressed violence that lies beneath the surface of his unfulfilled dreams. Overcome by this latent violence, Homer attacks an insufferable child star, Adore Loomis, at a movie premiere. Homer's attack moves this mob of dreamers and "starers" to archetypal mass violence and comprehensive destruction.

THE TITLE

Sources Of The Title

Like most of West's carefully selected titles, *The Day of the Locust* is a title with a core of symbolic reference. The title derives its meaning from several different sources, and it suggests a variety of illuminating interpretations. The most obvious source of reference to the locusts is the Bible. In the Old Testament (Exod. 10:3–6 and 13–15) Pharaoh's heart is hardened against the people of Moses, and when Pharaoh vows to keep the people in bondage, an east wind brings upon the land a plague of locusts. These insects wreak apocalyptic devastation until a west wind sweeps them all into the Red Sea. In the New Testament (Rev. 9:3–11) a scourge of locusts issues from a bottomless pit, and with the sting of scorpions they torment for five months all those who "have not the seal of God in their foreheads." Suffering from the scorpion-stings of the locusts, these men "shall desire to die, and death shall flee from them."

There are, however, at least two non-biblical sources for West's title. One of these is the title of a book by Gilbert Seldes, *The Years of the Locust* (1933). The other source is a passage from the concluding section of Archibald MacLeish's book of combined poetry and photography, *The Land of the Free* (1938). Since both of these books were well known at the time of their publication, and since West was highly conversant with the work of both writers, there is every likelihood that West was aware of these potential sources of reference as he winnowed all the possibilities in search of the best title for his novel in 1939.

The Years of the Locust has for a subtitle (America, 1929–1932). An examination of the first years of the Great Depression, it assumes that if one can explain the real significance of contemporary signs of the times, like the widespread use of the "raspberry" or the "bronx cheer" and the songs of Rudy Vallee, one can also explain the essential causes of cultural and economic chaos. Many of Seldes' most pertinent assumptions about the era - which was the era of West's novel also - can be used almost as a gloss upon the novel. Seldes says, for instance, "The search for a scapegoat, the witch hunt, is not only a terrifying element in all religions based on superstition; it occurs inevitably when disaster unsettles the minds of men" (p.15). This is one deep-rooted explanation of the actions of the destroying mob at the end of the novel. Again, in discussing the radical shifts in merchandising, Seldes compares actual conditions with those in a play by Bernard Shaw, wherein "the whole purpose of industry was to create ultimate rubbish" (p. 25). In West's novel the vast "dream dump" of Hollywood can easily be seen as no more "unreal" than the stockpiling of the "ultimate rubbish" which Shaw had envisioned as one of the real dangers in contemporary economic systems.

In the concluding passages of Macleish's *The Land of the Free*, after dramatizing the paradoxical plight of poverty-stricken Americans, the poet considers the possibility that the American dream has really been only "the singing of locusts out of the grass to the West," even though "the West is behind us now: / The West wind's away from us." Beyond the intriguing question of whether Nathanael West's fondness for puns might have focused his attention upon the possible double-meanings in his own name and MacLeish's references to the West wind, these queries lead to the ultimate question of whether, as the poet suggests, "the dreaming is finished."

Meaning Of The Title

Both of the biblical passages refer to plagues of locusts that have been visited upon mankind as scourges. In the Old Testament passage the locusts are a scourge upon those who deny freedom to the Chosen People, but in the New Testament the locusts are a scourge upon all those who, because they have rejected God, must suffer unbearable torment without being allowed to die - just as Tod Hackett cannot have the surcease of death, but must live on as the embodiment of a siren wailing the lostness of modern Man in a self-made wasteland. There is little doubt that West knew these biblical passages well and that he fully intended the biblical locusts to represent the senseless, swarming mob of cheated dreamers who are packed outside a movie theater at the end of the novel. Waiting impatiently to see the famous stars at a movie premiere, the mob bursts through police lines to destroy at random. The image of the locusts is especially apt for this purpose, since the biological "time-clock" of these insects causes them to emerge cyclically and in astronomical numbers, whereupon they ravage the land without real provocation. In this they are like the hordes of nameless, faceless, and altogether anonymous people in *The Day of the Locust* who have "come to California to die."

These people are typical Americans who have come to Hollywood in the futile hope of fulfilling their preconceived vision of the American dream. These pilgrims form a great impersonal mass of individuals who are usually passive. But deep inside all of them festers a resentment that grows more and more volatile as they find that the dream they seek is only a fake and tinsel Hollywood dream instead of the real one. Like the swarming of locusts after long dormancy, these cheated people must swarm and destroy when their sense of cheat has festered to suppuration. Like the locusts, they scourge the land, destroying themselves at the same time. In the early drafts of the manuscript, West considered this **theme** so important to the story that he tentatively used as a title *The Cheated*.

At the time West was writing *The Day of the Locust*, he was probably aware also of the special relevance of the locust image in the title of the novel by Seldes and of the images in the crucial passage at the end of the book by MacLeish. It is particularly likely that he had in mind the lines by MacLeish, partly because MacLeish's volume was published only a year before West's book appeared, and partly because the whole thrust of MacLeish's theme - the argument that for many people the "American dream" had evaporated - added several dimensions to the significance of the title which West eventually settled upon for his last novel.

Importance Of The Title

Few American novelists have been as meticulous as Nathanael West in the matter of choosing the perfectly appropriate title. For each of his books he sought a title that serves as an unmistakable clue to the whole complex of meaning which arises from the story itself. He seems to have intended the title to be an essential part of that complex of meaning. While he was writing *The Day of the Locust*, West kept lists of ideas for the title. After writing some of them upon the manuscript during the process of composition, he tentatively settled upon *The Cheated*. But up until the time when he began work on the galley proofs he was still uncertain of the title. Some of the other titles he had considered were *The Grass-Eaters, Cry Wolf*, and *The Wrath to Come*. At one time he thought of using *Days to Come*, but he rejected that title when he discovered that Lillian Hellman had already used it. On the galley proofs, West settled upon *The Day of the Locust*, and from that moment he appeared satisfied with the title.

COMPREHENSIVE ANALYSIS OF THE TEXT

The General Setting

he overall action of *The Day of the Locust* takes place entirely in or at the outskirts of Hollywood during the early part of its heyday as the movie capital of the world during the late 1930s. At this particular time, America has just recovered from the Great Depression, and with the advent of the "big star" era, Hollywood has become the mecca for every person in America who feels that he has "talent" to offer as the prime marketable commodity of the celluloid dream factories. For this reason, every writer and artist, every actor and "entertainer," every confidence man, every self-seeking entrepreneur in America has gone or considered going to Hollywood. Moreover, Hollywood is the place where the untalented may go to alleviate their boredom by their proximity to the glittering personalities whom they see on the silver screen and about whom they read incessantly in the tabloids and fan magazines. To both the entertainers and the "watchers," therefore, Hollywood is more a world of the mind than a real place, and whenever the real world emerges from the fanciful one, its realness proves unbearably tawdry, banal, and superficial.

For the most part, the world of *The Day of the Locust* is a vast fake purgatory, the broad-spectrum middle-ground of Hollywood life. This world is suspended somewhere between the lower-depths world of bums, grifters, and borderline skid-rowers and the fabulous "paradise" of movie stars, producers, directors, and tycoons who live in fairy-tale mansions on Sunset Boulevard. In *The Day of the Locust* the reader sees little of these highest and lowest worlds in the Hollywood universe. The scene lowest on the social and economic scale is the permanent campground of Earle Shoop and Miguel on the outskirts of town. The scene nearest the fabulous Hollywood "dream" is that of the party which takes place in the "replica" of a Southern mansion owned by the screen writer Claude Estee. Otherwise the reader sees mostly the massive middle-ground environment of the movie "fringe people." In Hollywood, this is a unique social and economic class. These people live upon the "leavings" of the motion picture industry - upon temporary and one-shot jobs as writers, artists, cameramen, scene technicians; upon casual jobs as extras; and - most unreliable of all Hollywood occupations - upon the bit parts and specialty acts. These people are always "on call" but are seldom or never called.

Their environment is a real community that has been permeated in every seam by the fakery of the movies. We see nothing of the inside of Tod Hackett's office at the studio, but the scenery outside is dominated by movie-set streets. These thoroughfares are used mostly by elaborately and authentically costumed motion picture casts moving from set to set. At the beginning of *The Day of the Locust*, these streets are filled with the armies of the Napoleonic wars - essential trappings in the **epic** recreation of a great historical event. To the casual observer at this particular moment, these streets belong to the Europe of Napoleon, not to twentieth-century America at all. At another moment they could belong to almost any other historical era in almost any other part of the world. These streets appear to have no permanent real character of their own. Their identity belongs to the "shooting schedule" of the studio.

Yet the real habitations of Hollywood people seem to be just as bizarre and fanciful as are those of the movie sets. At the beginning of the novel, Tod Hackett has been in Hollywood less than three months, and he still finds the place "exciting." As he walks home through a succession of typical Hollywood neighborhoods, his artist's eye is sometimes intrigued but more often shocked or offended at the architectural bastardies that have been perpetrated in the name of modern dwellings.

It appears as though Hollywood architects have plundered the architectural styles of every conceivable foreign culture and of every historical era in order to make these structures appear to be anything besides what they really are: twentieth-century American homes in a twentieth-century American suburb of Los Angeles. There are dwellings that appear to be Tudor English, German, Swiss, Mediterranean, Egyptian, Japanese, Mexican, Samoan, and most varieties of Near Eastern, including the Arabian Nights versions. These structures may be pure replicas of castles, villas, temples, cottages, ranch houses, huts, and shacks, or they may be any possible combination or permutation of these. But they all have this in common, that they are made of lath, plaster, and paper instead of stone and brick or any of the permanent architectural materials which these structures try so obviously and so unsuccessfully to imitate.

Other novelists have sought to describe the almost insane mixture of architectural styles that seem to flourish in Los Angeles as nowhere else on earth. Except for Nathanael West, however, no writer has provided so graphic a picture of this fantastic jumble as has Aldous Huxley in the first few pages of *After Many a Summer Dies the Swan*, a science-fiction novel that was published in the same year as *The Day of the Locust*. Huxley's **protagonist** is Jeremy Pordage, a mild-mannered English historian who has just arrived in Los Angeles from England, and who is therefore totally unprepared for what he sees. After passing through the downtown area, he notices the architecture of the churches: "primitive Methodist churches built...in the style of the Cartuja at Granada, Catholic churches like Canterbury Cathedral, synagogues disguised as Hagia Sophia, Christian Science churches with pillars and pediments, like banks." Then, beyond other monstrosities - for example, a restaurant built to look like a seated bulldog - he comes to a more affluent section: "elegant and witty pastiches of Lutyens manor houses, of little Trianons, of Monticellos; light-hearted parodies of Le Corbusier's solemn machines-for-living-in; fantastic adaptations of Mexican haciendas and New England farms.... Gloucestershire followed Andalusia and gave place in turn to Touraine and Oaxaca, Dusseldorf and Massachusetts."

Setting: San Bernardino Arms

Of all the houses and apartment houses that Tod Hackett passes and observes during his evening's walk from work, none is in worse taste than his own apartment house, the San Bernardino Arms (familiarly called the "San Berdoo"). Though the building seems to him deceptively satisfactory compared with his original Los Angeles domicile at the Chateau Mirabella (the hustlers' hotel in "Lysol Alley"), the San Bernardino Arms is at the same time as unimaginative in basic design and as sickening in decoration as the worst of the apartment houses along the Pinyon Canyon road. The San Bernardino Arms is merely an elongated three-story stucco box with plain windows along the back and sides. The front, however, is an elaborate facade containing double windows inside Moorish columns. These windows are topped by Near Eastern or perhaps Russian lintels in the shape of turnips. In worse taste is the color combinations, which even the most undiscriminating eye perceives as little less than nauseating: the basic color is that of mustard, and the columns framing the windows are pink. There is little doubt that West intends the San Bernardino Arms to represent the most flagrantly tasteless and offensive class of apartment buildings that flourished prolifically all over Los Angeles at the time of the action in the novel.

Setting: Homer Simpson's "Cottage." Just as the San Bernardino Arms is intended to represent the cheapest and the most tasteless kind of Hollywood apartment house, Homer Simpson's "cottage" at the end of the Pinyon Canyon road represents the worst kind of architectural monstrosity that the high-pressure Los Angeles real estate agents can bully people into buying or renting - especially diffident people like Homer, people who rent a house only because they cannot cope with the overbearing tactics of the realtor. This was Homer's reason for renting his house.

The house is a "cottage" only in a very misleading sense. The structure has a thick, heavy-looking thatched roof made of artificial straw, so that the house has the general appearance of a large Irish cottage. But beyond this superficial appearance it has no resemblance to an Irish cottage at all. Inside, the house is a planless and incredible melange of decors. The living room is a tasteless imitation of Spanish motifs, with pink-flecked orange walls, red and gold armorial banners, a plaster-hulled and wire-rigged galleon on the mantel, and with both real and artificial cacti arranged together in Mexican pots inside the fireplace. Various electrical fixtures are shaped like galleons. The furniture is upholstered in red damask, and the legs of the couch are carved to look like fat monks. The room is dominated by a huge mahogany trestle table studded with bronze-headed nails.

The two bedrooms are exact duplicates of each other and are furnished in a random selection of "New England" furniture and decor: spool beds, Winthrop dressers, and the same picture in both rooms - a Connecticut farmhouse in wintertime, with the usual wolf roaming about in the snow.

The prevailing impression is that everything in the house is a poorly concealed fake. Everything has been made to look like something that it quite clearly is not. The "thatch" of the roof is not straw but some kind of thick paper composition made to resemble straw. The gumwood door is painted to look like fumed oak. The huge hinges have been stamped by machine but are supposed to look as though they have been forged by hand. Even the two identical "New England" dressers in the bedrooms have been carefully painted so that they look like pine that has been left unpainted.

Even the location of this "Irish cottage" - at the very end of the Pinyon Canyon road - emphasizes the artificiality of architecture. Above and beyond the house rise the sere brown hills that surround Hollywood, and the city can be seen spread out below the canyon. Though the intent of the architect may have been to blend the house with its natural surroundings, the natural surroundings here belong clearly to Southern California and are in no conceivable way like any landscape that ever existed in Ireland. For this reason the "cottage" is only an especially painful example of all the rest of the Hollywood fakery that Tod has observed on his walk home from the movie studio.

Setting: The Hotel In Iowa

The only scene that has a setting outside of Los Angeles is a "flashback" in chapter 8, wherein West provides the reader with an account of a traumatic experience that Homer had during his twenty years as the bookkeeper at a hotel in the small town of Wayneville, Iowa. The manager of the hotel had sent Homer to the room of a woman guest to demand that she pay her overdue bill. The woman was Romola Martin, an alcoholic. But she was still young and sexually attractive, especially to Homer, who could not hide his nervousness and embarrassment. When she began to sob, he had foolishly given her his wallet and had begun to caress her avidly but awkwardly. Interrupted by a telephone call from the housekeeper, Homer realized that he was impotent and could not respond to the girl's invitation to return to the bed. He had run out of the room and had never been able to find the girl again. This **episode** haunts Homer for the rest of his life, and the psychological effects of it help to explain his bizarre relationship with Faye Greener.

Setting: Claude Estee's Mansion

In the social, economic, and professional spectrum of *The Day of the Locust*, Claude Estee's mansion is as close as anyone ever gets to the palatial Hollywood homes that constitute the highest order of the residences that help to make up the "Hollywood dream." Claude's residence is in every architectural detail a copy of the old Dupuy mansion near Biloxi, Mississippi, and the essential features of the landscaping are typical of Southern colonial grounds, including boxwood hedges and honeysuckle. The swimming pool is a touch of Southern California, however, and the grotesque rubber horse at the bottom of the pool is pure Hollywood sensationalism and practical jokery. Claude's house is modest compared with "Pickfair" or any other truly lavish estate of the established stars and tycoons in the Hollywood firmament, and the people at Claude's party are for the most part run-of-the-mill studio employees like Tod Hackett. The whole party at Claude Estee's mansion is a low-key **parody** of the scandalous Hollywood "orgies" that people are always reading about in lurid detail by way of the exposes that appear in almost every issue of every movie magazine. The sheer boredom and banality of this party (especially the persistent movie studio "shop talk") is part of West's intentional mockery of this aspect of the "Hollywood dream."

Setting: Mrs. Jenning's House

As one facet of West's mocking account of the typically "orgiastic" Hollywood house party, the short scene that takes place in Audrey Jenning's elite "call house" is, if anything, even more dull than the party that was going on at Claude's house itself. Though the "call house" is an elegant institution of its kind, managed with discretion, impeccably furnished, and decorated in muted tones of gray, violet, and rose, the privately shown movie - intended to be very prurient - is trite, unimaginative, and altogether uninteresting.

Setting: The Barrooms

To Harry Greener, public barrooms are theaters where he can present himself in private and gratuitous performances, with the customers of the bars as captive audiences. One of the shortest but most revealing passages in *The Day of the Locust* is West's description of Harry's inventive ploys to force the customers of a bar to tolerate his high-intensity, autobiographical "dramatic readings," which are really a form of self-inflicted suffering. It is a monument to his virtuosity that he is rarely stifled or ejected by the habitues of these barrooms, even though many quiet drinkers would ordinarily resent being disturbed in what they consider their private retreats. These are apparently ordinary barrooms, where people go to drown or to share their sorrow, and Harry has found that these people make sympathetic audiences for his broad virtuoso performances.

Setting: The Undertaking Parlor

In most Hollywood novels funerals are comic events. Hollywood people attend funerals in much the same way as they attend parties. Large numbers of strangers appear at the ceremonies, most of them hoping to catch a glimpse of some famous star, or at least yearning to see an uncontrollable display of emotion. Most of them want to be part of something bizarre - anything to take them out of the boredom of their everyday lives. This is one manifestation of the latent violence which erupts at the end of *The Day of the Locust.* Indeed, the actions of the mob at the end of the novel are foreshadowed by the actions of the embittered old people who hurry away from Harry's funeral in the hope of catching a glimpse of a famous movie star in another place.

The nearly insane unreality of Hollywood funerals has been captured best in Evelyn Waugh's *The Loved One* (1948). But in the description of Harry Greener's funeral Nathanael West manages to preserve just the right kind of spectacle and the right degree of irreverence to help the novel to its conclusion.

As Carolyn See remarks in her doctoral dissertation upon the Hollywood novel, Harry Greener's "co-tenants treat the funeral as a party, while the strangers watch it as pure spectacle. This refusal to look at death for what it really is, the refusal to show the proper awe, respect, sympathy or whatever is called for, is strong enough in *The Day of the Locust* to qualify as genuine mass dementia."

Setting: The Saddlery Store

Hodge's Saddlery Store is only one of the regular places of business along Sunset Boulevard. It is distinguished from other stores only by the fact that the motion-picture cowboys, bit players and stunt men, use the street outside the store as a gathering place. Earle Shoop habitually spends all day standing in front of the big display window. The central object of display in the window is a large, elaborately wrought Mexican saddle. Around it are arrayed all the smaller "tack", including some cruel-looking bits and spurs. On a rear shelf is a row of high-heeled cowboy boots. Of the interior of the store the reader sees nothing beyond these boots.

Habitually, Earle Shoop stands facing the street in front of this window, and at precisely measurable intervals he rolls a cigarette and lights it from a match ignited upon the tight-stretched fabric of his blue jeans. Except for this thirty-minute ritual he does only one thing: he stares unwaveringly at a malted milk sign on the roof of the building across the street.

This highly limited scene is the only glimpse the reader gets of the typical downtown area of Hollywood, and from what the reader sees here he can infer that the everyday world of downtown Hollywood is very little different from the downtown area of any other city in the United States. This is one of the paradoxes and disappointments of the "Hollywood Dream" - that one of the most famous street intersections in the world, Hollywood and Vine, is and has always been visibly indistinguishable from any other intersection in any ordinary city of America.

Setting: The Campground

Earle Shoop and Miguel live in a permanent camping ground that is far enough outside the environs of the city to eliminate any harassment by the city authorities. To reach the camp, Faye has to drive to the end of a city street and go the full length of a dirt road. At this point a visitor to the campground must leave the automobile in order to follow a series of footpaths up and down two or three arid canyons to a small valley filled with grass, brush, and trees. In this valley is the camp, which contains a shack built hastily of stolen tin highway signs. In contrast to the careless construction of the shack there is also a row of solidly and carefully built chicken coops. These coops contain Miguel's fighting cocks.

This campground reveals the social and economic status of Earle and Miguel, of course, but to Nathanael West the camp represents something even more germane to the general significance of the novel: this camp is the only setting in the story where the characters must react to "natural" phenomena as opposed to the purely man-made world of Hollywood and all that world stands for. To Earle and Miguel the things of nature are merely utilitarian. The trees and bushes are only firewood, the quail, rabbits, and other animals are only food to be caught, if possible, and eaten. The legalities of civilization - game laws, for instance - mean nothing. When Earle takes a quail alive out of a trap he is altogether unaware of its delicate beauty. He pulls its head off, drops the bird into a sack, and plucks it as he walks along. At camp he eviscerates the birds, snips them into quarters with tin snips (while Faye covers up her ears to shut out the sound), wipes them with a rag, and drops them into a pan of hot and sputtering lard.

To both Tod and Miguel the champion fighting cock seems beautiful. But to Tod the beauty of the bird lies in its gorgeous plumage, while to Miguel its beauty resides in its inbred fierceness. The cock is more a man-made thing than a creature that belongs in these natural surroundings, with the quail and wild song-birds. Tod perceives in the songs of the wild birds a haunting beauty, and though the birds are not conscious of the fact, their songs are full of tones that have meaning only for human beings, for civilized creatures, for the city-dwellers: sadness, melancholy, weariness. The birds do not feel these human emotions, but Tod hears them in the songs.

The only other wild thing in the novel is the lizard that lives in Homer Simpson's back yard, between the patio and the hills which rise behind the house. Much as Tod perceives the wild birds in terms of human traits, Homer identifies himself strongly with the lizard as it hunts flies. In *The Day of the Locust*, most wild things are seen as a reflection of and a commentary upon "civilized" human beings.

Setting: The Movie Studio

The scene outside Tod's office window at the beginning of the novel - the soldiers of the Napoleonic wars going from movie set to movie set - is an effective **foreshadowing** of the later scene in which Tod roams through the movie lots in search of Faye

Greener. To Tod, these authentically equipped and costumed soldiers appear to be real soldiers, just as everything false on the movie lots seems to be the real thing, even when broken, cast aside, or out of context. The movie lots represent the ultimate loss of distinction between appearance and reality.

In chapter 18 of *The Day of the Locust*, Tod Hackett deliberately goes upon a lone expedition through the movie lots, trying to find Faye Greener, who is working as an extra in the filming of a movie titled "Waterloo." In order to reach the back lot where the filming is taking place, Tod has to wander through any number of other movie sets. Some of these sets, as for instance a replica of the Sahara Desert containing a papier-mache Sphinx, are just being built and are as yet unfinished. Others, like a Western town, a Paris street that lies on the other side of the swinging doors of the Western saloon, and a Greek temple with the god Eros lying in a pile of rubbish, are old sets that are no longer being used for filming. Some of these scenes, like that containing a group of people on a picnic beside a cellophane waterfall, are actually being filmed, and members of the company keep Tod away. Scattered everywhere are things totally out of context: a canvas ocean liner with real life boats, an Arab on a white stallion followed by a truck loaded with snow, the superstructure of a huge blimp, a Trojan horse, and a set of palace stairs that rises from weeds and ends against a tree. He also sees an enormous dumping ground of movie sets and old properties - literally a vast "dream dump."

When Tod sees a number of cavalry soldiers in the uniforms of Victor Hugo's regiments, he knows that he is very close to the set where "Waterloo" is being filmed. He knows because he had done some costume drawings for these costumes, using Victor Hugo's descriptions from the account in *Les Miserables*. As the title of the movie suggests, this production is intended as an **epic** motion picture of the Napoleonic wars, culminating in an explicit re-enactment of Napoleon's defeat at Waterloo. Part of the action is the crucial attack on Mt. St. Jean. For this full-scale defense of the English against the French forces the set designers and production men have constructed a facsimile of Mt. St. Jean out of boards and canvas. Not knowing that the grips and carpenters are still working on the unfinished mock-up of the mountain, an assistant director orders the French cavalry to charge up the slope, and under the weight of horses and men the whole mountain collapses, sending large numbers of "soldiers" to the hospital. This scene represents the height of the confusion between appearance and reality during Tod's expedition through the various movie lots.

Setting: The Movie Premiere

The climactic scene in *The Day of the Locust*, and the concluding one, is the gathering of the enormous crowd outside Kahn's Persian Palace theatre. This scene takes place in a section of "downtown Hollywood," but West is careful to keep the reader from feeling that the action of the scene occurs in any specific physical location. The central location is the area in front of a theatre that is an obvious counterpart of Grauman's Chinese, where big Hollywood premieres are traditionally held. Otherwise, the area is an abstraction of Hollywood theatres. The area is less a physical location than an implicit extension of everything the "dream factories" represent in the lives of the people who are gathered there.

These spectators have gathered for the world premiere of some new motion picture, and their fiercest hope is that they might get close enough to the street entrance to see one or more of the stars of the new picture as the celebrities enter the theatre.

Most people have seen such premieres only in the newsreels or newspaper photographs, with the huge searchlights penetrating high into the sky, with the title of the picture in enormous letters on a brilliantly lighted marquee, and with a corps of special police officers holding back the roped-off crowds as the stars escort each other across the sidewalk from limousines parked at the curbside.

The crowd in *The Day of the Locust* has all of these glamorous trappings, but it is the largest of all such crowds. The nearly hysterical radio announcer estimates the crowd at ten thousand people, with others arriving every moment. These are all the bored, disappointed, and embittered middle-class people who have discovered that they are being cheated by the "Hollywood dream." Individually they are passive, but as part of the growing mob they become more and more angry and violent. Triggered by the spectacle of Homer Simpson insanely stomping Adore Loomis, the crowd releases its pent-up violence in a sudden frenzy, from which Tod is rescued only with the help of the police. This scene represents a form of apocalypse which justifies the critics in describing *The Day of the Locust* as an "apocalyptic novel."

Viewpoint: Limited Omniscience

The prevailing point of view from which Nathanael West relates the events of *The Day of the Locust* is that of the omniscient narrator. As the author of the novel, West takes advantage of a long-standing **convention** of storytelling which allows the writer of fiction to assume the position of an all-knowing observer who can tell the reader all he needs to know about all the characters in the story, including their emotions and thought processes. This all-knowingness is conventionally and logically the exclusive "privilege" of the omniscient narrator. But in *The Day of the Locust* West deliberately limits his authorial omniscience to the "centers of consciousness" of two main characters: Tod Hackett and Homer Simpson. Because all omniscient narratives are related in the third person, each of these characters becomes what Wayne C. Booth has called a "third person reflector" of the omniscient narrator. As such, each character is an agent through which the omniscient narrator chooses to reveal whatever he wishes to make known about all the other characters.

Mixed Omniscience

In this novel, however, West does not seem to have managed the limiting of the omniscient point of view as consistently as he might have done, and many critics have charged him with confusing the reader by using the viewpoint too loosely. They point out that the limited omniscience remains with Tod Hackett for the opening section of the novel, that it shifts to Homer for a second large section of the narrative, that it then returns to Tod and alternates awkwardly and unpredictably between the two for the rest of the story - sometimes resorting to small sections of general omniscience - and by this awkward mixture of viewpoints confusing the reader.

Confusion Of Viewpoints

This confusion does not arise merely from the fact that West has used more than one character as the "center of consciousness." Several important writers have successfully limited the use of the omniscient viewpoint to two or more "centers of consciousness". Henry James is notable as the most important pioneer in this kind of experimentation, and the use of multiple "third person reflectors" of the authorial persona has increased in recent years (as in much of the fiction of William Faulkner, and as in the "flexible" use of viewpoint in Joseph Heller's *Catch-22*). There is nothing innately confusing, then, in an omniscient narrator's using several "centers of consciousness" to tell a story. The technique is confusing only when the author uses the technique in confusing ways.

In order to sustain a clear and believable point of view, a writer of fiction must maintain a clear distinction between his own omniscient observations and those of the character to whose viewpoint the omniscience has been limited. Yet, as several critics and reviewers have pointed out, this distinction is not always clear in *The Day of the Locust*. It is unclear, for instance, whether the last paragraph in chapter one is to be attributed to West as the omniscient author or to Tod Hackett, who had already been established as the "third person reflector" of the omniscient author. Further, it is important for a novelist to avoid violating the "privilege of omniscience" by allowing a fictional character to know something that he cannot logically have knowledge of. Yet from time to time in *The Day of the Locust* West appears to violate this privilege, as he does in chapter fourteen when Tod - apparently listening to the songs of the quail and perceiving melancholy in the notes - appears to know that one of the singing birds is a trapped bird. Inasmuch as he and Earle have not yet checked the traps, Tod has no way of knowing that this particular bird is trapped, and the reader is at least momentarily confused.

A few critics have tried to defend West's uses of viewpoint in *The Day of the Locust*, but in general the critics have agreed that these violations of conventional practice have kept the novel from achieving the necessary unity. Unfortunately, even if one argues that West intended the novel as a generalized and symbolic depiction of a world in the process of winding down, and that therefore it should not be subjected to the conventional analysis accorded the dramatization of a particular character or problem, most critics appear to feel that these shifts are confusing to a reader and must be considered a failure in the use of viewpoint. By and large, it is commonly understood that these unfortunate shifts in viewpoint constitute the most serious weakness of *The Day of the Locust* as a novel.

In the early versions of the novel, West had told the whole story in the first person from the point of view of Claude Estee. But his editors suggested changes that eventually led West to use Tod Hackett and Homer Simpson as the two principal "centers of consciousness" for a story told mostly by means of "limited omniscience." It seems likely that any awkwardness in the use of viewpoint came from West's attempt to make such an extensive alteration in the basic viewpoint which he had already used in early versions of the manuscript.

Major Themes

In *The Day of the Locust* West has developed at least ten major themes, each theme emerging along with others, and each working with others to make, ultimately, a series of important statements about the place of the individual in American life during the first half of the twentieth century. A "**theme**" must be differentiated from the concept of what a novel is "about." This novel is "about" these themes, of course, but in a specific rather than a general sense. Otherwise, the novel is "about" a young Hollywood screen writer, Tod Hackett, who becomes personally involved with a grotesque group of Hollywood people, and whose relationship with them forces him to become a spectator of and to some extent a participator in their lives, as a consequence of which some things happen that change his own life drastically. But this is the basic subject of the novel. As Tod and Homer move through the action of the novel, certain things happen that make a form of commentary upon the meaning or lack of meaning in the events. These things may be crystalized as statements about the significance of the subject matter, and in the form of statements they become **themes** which, in turn, have an influence upon other aspects of the novel. Hyman, for instance, points out that the literary techniques which West uses in *The Day of the Locust* tend to grow out of his themes, just as the themes are responsible for the humor of the book (Nathanael West, pp. 42–43).

Ten Major Themes

It is possible to identify at least ten major themes that emerge from *The Day of the Locust*, and they may be listed as follows:

1. The modern world is a wasteland.

2. In this wasteland nothing is what it appears to be.

3. In the modern world all human pretense to greatness and nobility is absurd.

4. The average American has been cheated all his life by the unfulfilled promises of the "American Dream," of which the "Hollywood Dream" is the epitome.

5. Those people who "come to California to die" have never lived.

6. Those who have been cheated of their dreams are passive as individuals, but as soon as they form a large crowd they are possessed of uncontrollable violence.

7. In twentieth-century America this submerged violence always has some connection with suppressed sexual desires.

8. A necessary state of self-consciousness brings an awareness of the meaninglessness of life.

9. Few things in life are sadder than the truly monstrous.

10. Life imitates art.

Illustrations Of Major Themes

The following analysis will give you a better understanding of how the ten major **themes** are treated in the novel.

1. The "wasteland" **theme** in *The Day of the Locust* takes its phrasing from the central **theme** of T.S. Eliot's poem "The Waste Land" (1922). Indeed the connection is so close that several critics have uncovered direct parallels between West's novel and Eliot's poem. It has been argued, for instance, that in *The Day of the Locust* Tod Hackett functions in much the same way as Tiresias, the blind seer, functions in the poem: that is, as a dispassionate observer and prophet of impending disintegration. This is only one variation upon the many-sided aspects of Tod as the biblical prophet Jeremiah - a concept which makes of the novel a form of "Jeremiad," or a book of prophecies.

At any rate, the novel is full of images that support the "wasteland" **theme**, particularly the symbolic force of the great "dream dump" of old and useless stage sets (pure waste) that Tod sees during his expedition through the studio. This vast dumping ground of dreams becomes a counterpart of the wasteland of dreams which the world has become for modern man.

2. One of the signal characteristics of the modern wasteland is that in contemporary life there is everywhere a disparity between appearances and reality. In *The Day of the Locust*, West gives the reader prolific evidence that there is very little in the "Hollywood Dream" aspect of the "American Dream" that really is what it seems to be. The actors outside Tod's office at the beginning of the novel seem authentic people from another time and place, but they are counterfeits in the same way that everything on the movie sets is a counterfeit of what it seems to be. Outside the studios the houses are built in the architecture of other times and places. People on the street appear to be dressed for one purpose but are pursuing some other activity altogether. Indeed, most of the people are not what they seem. Claude Estee and Harry Greener are specific persons, but they have no identity beyond an endless succession of assumed roles. Faye Greener is "functionally" beautiful, but beneath and beyond this there is, at best, emptiness. Earle Shoop, who looks like a cowboy movie hero, is actually flat and dimensionless. This list could go on and on. But the important thing is to recognize that the modern wasteland is a wasteland partly because it is a world in which people are being incessantly cheated by appearances that supersede the realities which these people feel they have a right to believe in.

3. In the twentieth century, human beings appear to have lost the capacity to attain true dignity or heroic stature, since the values of our culture have had a leveling influence upon the individual rather than making it possible to exalt persons above the common. In *The Day of the Locust*, with its Hollywood setting, these leveling forces are exaggerated; yet the people in the story persist in seeing themselves as better and even as nobler than they are. Tod Hackett sees himself as an important painter and as a Jeremiah in art; Faye Greener sees herself as a fine actress; Harry Greener sees himself as a great comic; Abe Kusich sees himself as a man of physical strength and force, of cunning and insight; and so on. In every instance, however, these people are rendered absurd by visions of their own human stature that are patently far beyond their power to achieve - partly because in the modern world there is little greatness even in the stature they yearn for, and partly because their visions are manifestly self-delusions. If the characters are not made to seem absurd by these delusions, the delusions themselves are absurd.

4. One of the strongest **themes** in *The Day of the Locust* asserts that the "average" American has been cheated all his life by expectations to which he feels he has had the right, but which can never be fulfilled. For these people, Hollywood is the catalyst. According to standard versions of the "American Dream," one must work hard all his life at some dull and spiritually unrewarding occupation in order at last to enjoy ease, leisure, and satisfaction in some place that offers all the "American Dream" has fed their imagination upon: a soothing sea, opulent groves of oranges and grapefruit, warmth in the everlasting sunshine, lack of worry. Moreover, every day,

all their lives, they have been led to expect entertainment in the forms made most familiar to them by newspaper, magazine, newsreel, and motion pictures - that is, the sheer excitement of limitless sex in the sun, romance, intrigue, cowboys-and-Indians, cops-and-robbers, and all the "glamor" epitomized by the dreamworld that is Hollywood. Hollywood, then, is a microcosm of everything in the "American Dream" for which these people have yearned but which they can never have. As Walter Allen says (*The Modern Novel*, p. 171), "West's locusts are the middle-class retired middle-aged who have crawled from Iowa to die in exacerbated boredom in a Never-Never Land that has deceived them."

5. The most obvious and in many ways the most disturbing thing about these people who have "come to California to die" is that they are actually seeking to come alive for the first time after spending their lives in mental, emotional, and spiritual deadness. Except for those who gather briefly at Harry Greener's funeral and then leave to look for more potent possibilities of excitement, the reader of *The Day of the Locust* sees little of these people in groups until the end of the novel. But in Homer Simpson as an individual one sees the very type and symbol of those who make up the locust-hordes that have swarmed to California in search of the life-dream they have never been able to live. Like Homer, these people are in a state of mental, emotional, and spiritual paralysis akin to death, or at best akin to the chrysalis stages of suspended animation that precede emergence as a full-blown creature - in the form of locusts, for instance. One of the frightening things about this concept is its implicit universality. The phenomenon cannot be confined to Hollywood, though by the nature of Hollywood it is more

volatile there. The same kind of apocalyptic convulsion that ends *The Day of the Locust* could occur in any place where astronomical numbers of those "living dead" of the modern wasteland-world might gather to fulfill the dreams of which they have been cheated.

6. In *Nathanael West: The Ironic Prophet* (p. 117) Comerchero argues that the America of *The Day of the Locust* is schizoid." Two divergent forces were at work: idealism and resentment. The inevitable conflict between these antagonistic tendencies is aggravated by the crowd's inability and lack of desire to fathom the forces at work upon it. The result is a savage sense of betrayal that must erupt in violence." Yet only in a large crowd can this sense of betrayal erupt in violence. It is the nature of mob psychology that large crowds tend to coalesce in the mass all the dark and suppressed things which separate individuals - apart from the mass - are altogether incapable of recognizing in themselves, let alone putting them into any form of overt action. So it is with the people of *The Day of the Locust*. Like Homer with his compulsion to sleep as in death, with his fear of dark spaces between street lights, with his almost cosmic apathy, with his indecisiveness - like Homer, the people who make up the crowd at the movie premiere are passive, ineffectual, even self-effacing as individuals. But absorbed into the mob, without individual identity, they feel and can act out only their shared sense of betrayal. The eruption of violence is inevitable under these conditions.

7. Whatever combination of factors may be responsible for the eruption of violence under these circumstances, the long suppression of sexual drives in the lives of modern human beings is one of the constant factors and one of the

most virulent. In *The Day of the Locust*, Faye is a sexual locus around which the lives and emotions of the men revolve, and in Tod's apocalyptic painting he has depicted her as pursued by all these men, as well as by a horde of utter strangers. Out of this sexually dominated locus emerges Homer Simpson, whose deeply suppressed sexual drives are brought to life and simultaneously destroyed by Faye's sexual promiscuity. Precipitated by these events into a state of insane distraction, he unleashes his pent-up fury upon a tormentor under just the right circumstances to set up a chain reaction in the crowd at the movie premiere. The extent to which the mob violence springs from various kinds and degrees of sexual repression is made clear to the reader by the recurrent **episodes** of exploitive sex that occur as part of the composition of the crowd, while men and women are crushed helplessly together and are moving rhythmically with the ebb and flow of the human tide.

8. In the Westian world, the absurd and the meaningless are essential conditions of modern life, and it is important that the people in *The Day of the Locust* attain an awareness that the lives they lead and the dreams they may have are merely part of a world in which everything is reduced ultimately to a state of absurdity and meaninglessness. The only protection these people have against the delusion that their lives are meaningful is a deliberately sustained attitude of self-consciousness that lets them see their lives in the perspective afforded by a world in which the absurd and the meaningless are necessary elements. For most of the characters in this novel, the "masks" they wear help to establish this perspective. In Tod Hackett this deliberately fostered consciousness of self is very strong, as if evinced by his relentless attempts to see himself and his world clearly

and objectively in his projected painting of "The Burning of Los Angeles."

9. Through the constant tension between the comic and the serious in this novel, a **theme** arises that asserts the pervasive pathos of the monstrous in the modern world. West states this **theme** explicitly in the last sentence of the first chapter, and for him the statement is partly a declaration of the difference between the comic and the pathetic in this novel. It is only incidental to West's statement that in the history of literary criticism, as far back as the mid-eighteenth century, Henry Fielding had already argued that the monstrous is not legitimately an object of comedy. To West, however, the principle is somewhat more subtle and complex. In describing the grotesque architecture of Pinyon Canyon Road, he suggests that some things appear comic that are really pathetic, that it is difficult to laugh at a tasteless attempt to create beauty or to aspire to romance, but that it is "easy to sigh." To West, therefore, the truly monstrous is less likely to be horrible than it is to be merely "sad." Further, though West does not say so explicitly, everything in *The Day of the Locust* indicates that to the author the grotesque is very like the monstrous in the same sense - something more sad or pathetic than comic.

10. The idea that "life imitates art" is a form of paradox: we normally think, "art imitates life." The mimetic or imitative or representational function of the arts is a concept of such ancient and persistent vintage that any reversal of the principle seems at first a sheer self-contradiction. Yet, as Oscar Wilde most cleverly and convincingly demonstrates in "The Art of Lying, "the essential truth of art becomes in time the truth of real

life. In *The Day of the Locust* West gives ample evidence that in the modern American culture this principle is everywhere operative. The real people in Hollywood have become in many ways indistinguishable from life in the motion pictures. Homer Simpson is described as resembling one of Picasso's archetypal human figures. An explicit illustration of the principle is the fact that the painting which Tod conceives in his creative imagination actually becomes reality at the end of the novel. In West's novels, however, it is frightening to notice that the art which life now imitates is not "great art" or "classic art" or "traditional art" but frequently "pop art." In the modern world, popular culture tends to imitate popular art.

Motif Distinguished From Theme

Though they are related to each other in their general function, **themes** and motifs are not the same. A motif is not a statement of meaning, except in the sense that a clause or a phrase or some other verbal unit may be repeated throughout a literary work from time to time, so that the recurrence of the verbal unit turns it into a motif (or as the repetition of a phrase in fiction and drama is sometimes called, a leitmotif). Otherwise, a motif is ordinarily the significant recurrence throughout a literary work (and in a larger sense throughout groups of similar literary types) of a special kind of character, incident, object, action, or literary device. The significance of a motif usually arises from the patterned recurrence of the motif rather than from the literary element constituting the thing that recurs, though the recurrent device itself can have some descriptive, symbolic, or thematic value of its own. The appearance of various motifs in *The Day of the Locust* is discussed along with symbols in the Sectional Analysis and Interpretation of the Text.

Characters

The entries in this section are primarily critical descriptions of the characters that appear in *The Day of the Locust*. For analyses of methods of characterization and functions of the characters as part of the narrative, see part B in the Sectional Analysis and Interpretation of the Text.

Calvin

A movie cowboy. He stands in front of Hodge's saddlery store with Earle Shoop, wearing the standard cowboy actor's costume of big hat and cowboy boots, and he carries a paper valise tied together with a rope. Habitually, he sits on his haunches and chews a twig. He argues about Mexicans as a race with Chief Kiss-my-Towkus. It is from Calvin's point of view that the reader gets the report of the fight at the party in the canyon.

Miss Carlisle

The room clerk at the hotel in Iowa, where Homer Simpson was the bookkeeper.

Chief-Kiss-My-Towkus

A wrinkled movie Indian with a purple tongue, broken orange teeth, and long hair held down by a beaded strap. He carries a sandwich board sign advertising Tuttle's Trading Post, and while bantering with Tod and Calvin he makes jokes in bad Jewish dialect. The "Chief" is violently anti-racial, especially with regard to all Mexicans.

Mary Dove

One of Mrs. Jenning's call girls, and a close friend of Faye Greener. With Mary's help, Faye becomes one of Mrs. Jenning's girls also. Note the **irony** in the combined names - that of the Holy Mother coupled with that of an archetypal symbol of purity and innocence.

Claude Estee

A successful Hollywood screen writer whose house is a facsimile of the old Dupuy Mansion of Biloxi, Mississippi. Having lost his personality in his craft, he has no personality of his own and must take upon himself all the **cliche** characters he has created for the motion pictures. His idea of a sophisticated joke is to submerge a rubber replica of a dead horse in his swimming pool. His idea of special entertainment for his party guests is the showing of a pornographic movie at Mrs. Jenning's house.

The Gingoes

An Eskimo family brought to Hollywood for retakes of a polar exploration movie. Refusing to go back to Alaska, the Gingoes remain in Hollywood, where they have been good friends of Harry Greener, with whom they liked to share their own peculiar ideas of food. They appear at Harry's funeral, sit in the front row, and try to be the first to view Harry's corpse, but are deterred by Mrs. Johnson.

Faye Greener

A platinum blonde Hollywood extra, perhaps modeled upon the real figure and character of the now legendary screen star Jean Harlow.

She is the daughter of Harry Greener. She accepts casual dates from Earle Shoop and is the "friend" of Tod Hackett, whose avid attempts to become her lover she keeps on an impersonal plane because he cannot offer either good looks or wealth. Later she is the permanent house-guest of Homer Simpson, is the lover of the Mexican Miguel, and is a call girl for Mrs. Jenning. Her sexual passage with Miguel in the bedroom of Homer's house precipitates Homer's insane distraction and is therefore indirectly the cause of the riot at the end of the novel. She is the central figure of one grouping in Tod's projected painting of "The Burning of Los Angeles."

Harry Greener

An old-time vaudeville comic and the father of Faye Greener. Harry's "sole method of defense" against the real world is his incessant clowning. His entire character has been absorbed into the vaudeville tricks, stunts, routines, recitations, and devices that he has spent his life in perfecting, and he has lost the power to distinguish between real and simulated emotion, even inside himself. He compounds jars of "silver polish" at home and sells it from door to door. He is fond of cornering patrons of public barrooms in order to give them a form of "dramatic reading" of his life story. Through the onset of Harry's fatal illness in Homer Simpson's house, Homer and Faye Greener are first acquainted. Harry's death is Faye's reason for becoming one of Mrs. Jenning's call girls for a short period of time.

Tod Hackett

A young graduate of the Yale School of Fine Arts who has been hired by telegram to learn the designing of sets and costumes for a Hollywood movie studio. Physically he is big and sprawling, blue-eyed, and "almost doltish." Yet he is actually a complicated person "with a whole set of personalities, one inside the other, like a nest of Chinese boxes." To offset the lack of artistic challenge in his movie studio job, Tod is planning to paint an enormous masterpiece to be titled "The Burning of Los Angeles," depicting the revolt of all those who have "come to California to die," and using the figures of all his Hollywood friends and acquaintances.

Many critics regard Tod as the fictional counterpart of Nathanael West in this novel. None of these critics appears to have considered the likelihood that Tod's name has any symbolic or descriptive overtones as the names of central characters in West's other novels have had. It seems possible that his German-speaking cultural background has led him to couple together the grammatically explicit German word for death, "Tod," and the highly suggestive manufactured word "Hackett," from "hack," as in a literary or artistic "hack" such as West felt himself to be in his screenwriting capacity. If so, the name implies "the death of a hack" or even perhaps "a dead hack." In terms of Tod's character and situation this interpretation makes possible some illuminating overtones.

Hink

One of the movie cowboys who stand in front of Hodge's saddlery store. He has no big hat, perhaps having sold it, but he still has his boots. His face is completely covered with tiny wrinkles. He reminds one of an exercise boy at a racing stable.

Holsepp

The mortician and funeral director who owns the funeral parlor where Harry Greener's funeral is held.

Audrey Jenning

The madam of the Hollywood call-girl house where Claude Estee's guests watch a pornographic movie. Mary Dove is one of her girls, and later, for a short time, so is Faye Greener. Mrs. Jenning is a fair-haired, red-complexioned, generally handsome woman with smooth skin. She is sophisticated and has a faultless sense of decorum. Her "house" is a high-class establishment, impeccably designed and furnished. None of the girls lives at the house, and none of the actual "entertaining" of dates occurs on the premises. The "house" is a place where the girls are called, where the dates are arranged, and where the men may come to pick up their dates. For providing these tasteful and high-class services, Mrs. Jenning gets a considerable percentage of each fee.

Mrs. Johnson

The janitress at the San Bernardino Arms. She is an overbearing woman with a face "like a baked apple." Her hobby is making the formal arrangements for funerals and seeing that they are properly carried out. She plans and oversees arrangements for Harry Greener's funeral.

Abe Kusich

Known as "Honest Abe Kusich" - an aggressive, pugnacious dwarf who lives at the San Bernardino Arms. Abe is responsible for finding Tod his apartment at the "San Berdoo," and he becomes one of Tod's regular acquaintances, offering racing tips and other "inside" information of various kinds. Despite his tiny size, Abe has a powerful grip, little fear of full-sized men, and considerable personal courage. At the cock fight he ably "handles" the bird with the broken beak and is slammed against a wall by the Mexican Miguel, though he is not seriously hurt. Among his friends, Abe often displays his truculence as a form of joking and mere horseplay, though among those he does not like, the pugnacity is usually serious. Abe Kusich regards himself as an "expert" on almost everything in and around Hollywood.

Adore Loomis

One of the thousands of "talented" children in Hollywood who are being groomed as child stars in the movies. Adore, the son of Maybelle Loomis, is an eight-year-old boy with a pale face, shaped eyebrows, large forehead, and staring eyes. Except for a Buster Brown collar, he is dressed like a man. To annoy grown-ups he imitates the Frankenstein monster. As part of his repertoire he sings for Tod and Homer a sexy, suggestive blues song called "Mama Doan Wan' No Peas," using a husky blues-song voice and all the appropriate gestures, whose meaning he seems to understand. Adore's insufferably direct tormenting of Homer at the movie premiere causes Homer to stomp him in an insane rage, precipitating the riot.

Maybelle Loomis

A neighbor of Homer Simpson, and the mother of Adore Loomis. She is a widowed Hollywood housewife who is a follower of Dr. Know-All Pierce-All, leader of the "raw-foodists." She considers California paradise on earth, and like a horde of other mothers, she hauls her small son from studio to studio and sends him to a talent school, determined to make him a child movie star. Otherwise, she appears to be only an ordinary plump American housewife.

Marie, The "Bonne"

The central character in the pornographic movie that is shown to Claude Estee's party guests at Mrs. Jenning's. She is a buxom young French girl in a tight maid's uniform, and she is a servant to a middle-class French family, each member of whom desires her, though she desires only the young daughter of the family. The movie is full of boring situational **cliches** in which Marie hides members of the family one after another in her room before there is a series of mutual discoveries.

Romola Martin

An alcoholic young girl who is behind in her rent at the Iowa hotel where Homer Simpson is bookkeeper. Her childish, nervous mannerisms secretly excite Homer one day in the elevator, but he attributes his excitement to disgust. When Homer has to go to her room to ask her to pay her rent and leave the hotel, she begins to sob. After offering her his wallet, Homer caresses her impulsively until the telephone interrupts. After the phone call, when she offers herself to him, he runs out of the room. The next day she pays her bill and checks out of the hotel.

Miguel

A Mexican who shares the camp with Earle Shoop and who raises and fights the game cocks. He is dark-skinned, with big "Armenian" eyes and tight, curly, black hair. He usually wears a long-haired sweater, tennis shoes, and soiled duck trousers with a red bandanna for a belt. At the canyon party he sings and dances intimately with Faye, and after the cock fight in Homer's garage, Homer finds him in bed with Faye.

Joan Schwartzen

A female tennis champion who is a guest at Claude Estee's party. She is a big woman with large hands and feet, bony shoulders, and a prematurely aging skin, especially on her neck, though she has a pretty teen-age face. She appears to enjoy making what she considers outrageous remarks, especially with regard to sexual matters. At the party she attaches herself to Tod, demanding that he escort her to a group of men who seem to be telling off-color jokes. But when the talk turns out to be Hollywood "shoptalk" she takes him into the garden to show him the rubber horse in the swimming pool.

Earle Shoop

A movie cowboy extra and bit-player from a small Arizona town. He shares the canyon camp with Miguel, and when he is not working in the movies he spends his time standing in front of Hodge's saddlery store. Six feet tall, he becomes about six feet eight inches tall with his big Stetson hat and his high-heeled cowboy boots. With his narrow shoulders, lack of hips and buttocks, and straight thin legs, he seems "polelike." He has a round chin and round eyes, and a thin mouth at right angles to a straight nose. His skin is of a uniformly reddish tan hue. His face seems "two dimensional." He is a regular "date" of Faye Greener, who considers him, in the language of the fan magazines, "criminally handsome." He speaks in monosyllables and has no depth of character or personality, and he appears to be perpetually broke. He invites Faye to dinner, but takes her and Tod to the camp to eat wild quail that he has trapped. He precipitates the fight which disrupts the canyon party.

Homer Simpson

An ex-bookkeeper for a hotel in a small town in central Iowa. After twenty years at the hotel - where he had worked ten hours a day, eaten for two, and slept the rest of the time - he has come to California for a rest after catching pneumonia in the rain. He has saved about $16,000 from his work and a small legacy to afford him leisure in California, and he has rented an outlandish "Irish cottage" at the end of Pinyon Canyon Road, where he can sit alone in the back yard and watch a lizard trying to catch flies in a trash heap. Though he is often very sleepy, Homer is afraid to fall asleep because it is almost impossible for him to wake up, and he fears that he may not arise. In getting out of bed he moves like a badly made robot. His enormous hands, which appear to have a life of their own, separate from the rest of his body, always remain asleep for a long time, and he has to immerse them in cold water to bring them to life. He is a large man with heavy muscles and a full chest but a small head. Somehow, despite his size, he does not seem strong or virile. Having emotional cycles that surge up but never break, he has long periods when he is emotionally drained. If he walks the streets at night, he hurries in panic through the dark spaces and halts for breath under the street lights. He spends much of his time trying to avoid remembering the **episode** with Romola Martin. (This episode is recounted under the Martin entry.)

When Harry Greener becomes ill in his house while trying to sell Homer some "silver polish," Homer meets and becomes hopelessly but platonically infatuated with Faye, whom he pursues awkwardly with small gifts and rather pathetic attentions. After Harry's death, Homer makes an arrangement with Faye whereby he will take care of her until she becomes a star, whereupon she will repay him all the expenses with six percent interest. They are actually keeping records of expenditures for clothes and food. It is supposed to be a purely business arrangement, but its real effect upon Homer's emotional life is obvious when he becomes totally distracted and disintegrates emotionally after finding her in bed with Miguel.

Tone

Tone" is an indication - of the attitude which the author adopts toward the reader, and of the author's personal relationship with the reader. On the written page, tone is the equivalent of "tone of voice" in oral discourse. In *The Day of the Locust* there is a problem in differentiating among various tones because West has deliberately fused or combined two basically different tones - the comic and the pathetic - which together establish a prevailing tone that is almost indefinable because it contains elements of both. There is little doubt that the basic tone of this novel is in a general sense comic, and that more specifically the tone is "ironic" - a special variety of the comic which arises when there is a difference between what is asserted and what is actually true. One needs only to look on almost any page of *The Day of the Locust* to see the immense variety of ways in which West's prose achieves ironies and sustains a general tone of **irony** on both verbal and structural levels of the narrative. The comic tone shifts from time to time for special purposes within the narrative, as when the farcical tone becomes most appropriate to the description of the movie that is shown at Mrs. Jenning's. But the basic tone remains ironic. Combined with the tone of **irony**, and frequently almost indistinguishable from it, however, is a disturbing note of compassion that sustains a heavy tone of pathos. West creates this ironic-pathetic tone in the first chapter, and thereafter the novel is never entirely free from the peculiar tonal tension that prevails. This tonal fusion becomes most obvious at the end of the first chapter, where West writes, "Both houses were comic, but he didn't laugh." And the passage ends a few lines later with "But it is easy to sigh. Few things are sadder than the truly monstrous." In West's novels, this note of pathos is peculiar to *The Day of the Locust*. It does not appear in the other novels, and even in this one it sometimes gives way to a tone of sheer horror, as at the end of the novel.

Style

In recent years it has become necessary to distinguish between two concepts of style, each useful and applicable in its own sphere, but each so widely different in scope as to make it necessary for student and teacher to let each other know which sense of "style" one is using in any particular literary analysis or interpretation. One concept of style is what has become known as "the narrow view" - the view that style means "manner" and is concerned only with how a writer says what he says. The other concept of style is "the broad view" - the view that the writer's style consists of all the choices he makes during the act of composition. In our discussion here, we are concerned with "the narrow view," since any discussion of "the broad view" would involve all the individual sections that this study guide has broken up into divisions for clearer analysis and interpretation.

In "the narrow view," then, West's style is highly distinctive. Though it is full of shifts and subtleties that make it difficult to say precisely what the "Westian style" or manner is, there are certain basic characteristics and ingredients of his style that distinguish it from that of any other writer.

Brevity

Perhaps the most obvious characteristic of West's style is its compression. This compression is the result of West's tendency to rely upon short, concise units of expression, upon his monosyllabic words and short, concise sentences to achieve what is best described as a "spare" style. This style forces West to select rigidly by omitting non-essential ideas from his sentences, and it forces him to achieve his effects simply and directly, with little use of modification. The result is that West must choose his adjectives and adverbs very carefully and to be sure that each one is the most appropriate and colorful modifier possible, so that the modification achieves maximum effects with a minimal number of words. The result is an almost irreducible form of sheer economy in self-expression, and among modern American novelists West is supreme in this regard. The effect is perhaps best seen in his frequent use of what Comerchero (Nathanael West: *The Ironic Prophet*, p. 40) has called "the short terminal sentence" - the short, brutally blunt sentence that ends a train of thought. Once again, the last sentence of the first chapter of *The Day of the Locust* is a good example, though a dozen others could be found within as many pages.

Figurative Language

Another distinguishing characteristic of West's style is that it abounds in the use of similes, metaphors, and other figures of speech, even though the extreme economy of the style remains unchanged. Indeed, in some ways these figurative devices contribute to the brevity and economy of the style. West frequently uses these devices in the same way a poet does, to suggest as much as possible in as few words as possible. These techniques are probably a part of West's theory that novels can be written according to Poe's definition of a poem.

At any rate, West is capable of seizing upon whole groups of images and symbols that help to sustain the continuity of *The Day of the Locust*. An example of this is the complex of wasteland images, some of which West may have taken from Eliot, but most of which he uses in a unique fashion. The whole section upon the "dream-dump," for example, is part of just such a complex of imagery.

One can find razor-sharp individual **similes** and **metaphors** on almost every page, and whenever West writes without using them, the writing seems to lack much that makes the style distinctive. At random one finds this **simile**, for instance (*New Directions Edition*, p. 114): "Its song was like pebbles being dropped one by one from a height into a pool of water." And equally at random (p. 87) one finds West writing metaphorically of Homer's emotional states as "only the refuse of feeling."

Realistic Detail

Despite his dense use of figurative language, West relies wherever possible upon clear, concrete, realistic detail, and from time to time he renders an entire passage in a crisp, disciplined type of realistic narrative that competes well with the best examples one can find of the so-called "documentary school" of realism that flourished in the thirties. In *The Day of the Locust* West's narrating of the cock-fight **episode** is the most frequently used illustration of his capacity to write "realistically."

Parody

Among West's distinguishing features as a parodist is his capacity to use as **parody** the **diction** and the general style of well-known popular forms of discourse. In *The Day of the Locust*, in describing Faye's fascination with "success stories," for instance, West actually uses the **diction** and style of the "true romance" and the "confessional" types of pulp magazines. In fact, West not only uses this language here, but he uses it so opulently that it mocks itself and becomes an obvious **parody** of all such super-sensuous **diction** as it is used in the pulp magazines.

Experimentation And Polish

Much of West's uniqueness as a stylist is the result of the author's willingness to experiment with language in his search for ways to produce comic effects with his prose. His attempt to blend comedy and pathos is evidence of West's experimental approach to prose fiction, and the austerity of the style is itself the result of careful but courageous experimentation. Ultimately, whatever the specific characteristics of West's prose style may be, the unique quality of the style is probably the result of his infinitely careful polishing of detail. He not only worked and reworked his material endlessly, but he did so with discipline, with plan and judgment and control, working always toward clearly defined goals. In this respect, West is one of the most thoroughly disciplined of all modern American prose writers, and the effects of the polishing can be seen in every sentence. It becomes especially noticeable in long and complex sequences of narrative, as in the depiction of the riot at the end of the novel, where matters of rhythm, proportion, emphasis, pacing, and **climax** are of paramount importance. In this section of the novel West demonstrates the infinite care which he is capable of lavishing upon the most subtle and difficult materials of his craft, and the result is a style that can be called distinctively "Westian."

Plot Structure

The structure of the narrative in *The Day of the Locust* is closely connected with the fact that West intended the narrative to form a "short novel." It is, indeed, a "short novel," running to hardly more than a hundred and sixty pages in any published edition. Yet it is by far the longest of West's novels - more than twice as long as *Miss Lonelyhearts*, and a third again as long as *A Cool Million* - and the greater scope of *The Day of the Locust* appears to have caused West to use different structural devices while trying for the same over-all structural effects that he had already achieved in previous novels. The results may not have been as satisfactory as he had hoped.

Building his novels in general accord with Poe's prescriptions for a short poem, West managed to achieve in most of his earlier novels a compressed, steadily rising structure, with few if any digressions, eddies, or troughs, but moving directly toward a **climax** that ends the narrative without **denouement** or any falling-off of the action. The structure of these novels is straight-line and irrevocably rising, with gradual acceleration of pace and with swift, hard, clean **climax**. But however much the added length may add by way of greater substance, the larger scope of *The Day of the Locust* appears to have made it impossible for West to achieve quite the same focus, economy, and unity as he created in his earlier novels.

Critics have repeatedly questioned the structural necessity and utility of certain **episodes** in *The Day of the Locust*, pointing out that these scenes represent a less exacting selectivity than is characteristic of the earlier novels. The scene most often mentioned in this regard is the **episode** at Mrs. Jenning's. At any rate, *The Day of the Locust* appears to suffer from a loosening of structure that keeps it from attaining the same degree of unity and coherence that West successfully strove for in the other novels, and the structural effect is not as strong. As Comerchero describes the effect of the narrative structure in this novel (*Nathanael West: The Ironic Prophet*, p. 131): "A feeling of diffuseness and lack of compression results, and the novel fails to impress one with the power of the executioner's axe; instead, it leaves a series of vivid hatchet marks, each one clear and incisive."

THE DAY OF THE LOCUST

TEXTUAL ANALYSIS

SECTIONAL ANALYSIS AND INTERPRETATION OF THE TEXT

....

The Day of the Locust is divided into twenty-seven short chapters, each chapter headed by a numeral but with no chapter title or heading of any kind. One must assume that West preferred that the reader should infer the substance and purpose of each chapter from the material of the chapter itself, instead of having the "message" of the chapter broadcast to him at the beginning of the chapter, as is true of *Miss Lonelyhearts*. Functionally, however, the novel divides itself quite clearly into five sections, each section distinguishable as a separate functional unit in the overall narrative. In order to expedite and clarify the process of analysis and interpretation, this study guide will take advantage of these divisions in the narrative, using each division - or "set" of chapters - as the basis for detailed analysis and interpretation of the narrative. The extent of each section, the number of chapters in it, and an appropriate label or heading have all been provided for each section.

SECTION 1: TOD HACKETT, CHAPTERS 1-6

The six initial chapters of the novel can be called the "Tod Hackett" section, since in these chapters the omniscient persona of the author has largely confined the point of view to that of Tod Hackett. In this section, the reader sees Tod's world through Tod's eyes and feels toward that world, at least initially, as Tod feels. The section begins with Tod watching the movie soldiers outside his office window at quitting time, and it ends with Tod's thanking Homer for the gifts he has brought to Faye and to the dying Harry Greener. As Tod realizes that he has broken through Homer's dense and complex reserve, this division ends with the opening of chapter 7, where the viewpoint becomes primarily Homer's.

Setting

Though the general setting for the action of *The Day of the Locust* is Hollywood, the specific scenes in each section shift from place to place inside Hollywood or its immediate outskirts. In section 1 the opening scene occurs just outside Tod Hackett's Hollywood studio, where movie soldiers are going past the window. The setting then shifts to the streets of Hollywood as Tod walks homeward observing the costumes of the people and the architecture of the houses he passes. In chapter 2 the scene is largely Tod's former residence, the Chateau Mirabella, though it shifts to a scene in a drug store, where Tod meets Abe Kusich and decides to rent a room at the "San Berdoo." The scene in chapter 3 is Tod's room at the San Berdoo. In chapter 4 there is a radical shift to the party at Claude Estee's mansion, including a transitory scene at Mrs. Jenning's. Chapter 6 takes place altogether in the Greeners' apartment in the San Berdoo. As in most sections of the novel, there are rapid and frequent changes of scene within short spaces of time.

Viewpoint

All of section 1 is told in third person from the point of view of Tod Hackett by the omniscient "persona" of the author.

Exposition

The opening chapters of *The Day of the Locust* are excellent examples of the use of "integrated" **exposition**. Instead of beginning the novel with a block of expository details that establish time, place, character, and background, West provides these details one by one as the sequence of the action makes it necessary for the reader to know these basic introductory elements of the narrative. In other words, the **exposition** is going on all during the episodes, without the reader's being aware that expository material is being introduced. This method is by far the most subtle and difficult way of managing the **exposition,** but it is also the most effective when it is done well.

In the opening chapter of *The Day of the Locust* one is given two absolutely essential details of **exposition** in the first short paragraph: the introduction of a central character and the setting of a specific scene, which is the studio-artist's office facing upon an actor-filled studio street. After a concrete description of the street scene, West returns to his character and provides a background for his character's present situation. Then he switches the scene to the people and the houses of the Hollywood streets. From this point on, the details of setting are all part of the **exposition**, along with other details that West saves for the right time and place. Character-building goes on continuously but indirectly during the dialogues with Abe Kusich, the scenes concerning Faye Greener, the party at the Estees', the **episode** at Mrs. Jenning's, and the scenes in the Greeners' apartment before Homer becomes part of the scene.

From the opening scene, time sequences are established loosely but accountably, with periods of time traced by phrases like "a few days later," "it was after eight o'clock," "from then on," and so forth. The time-sequences are not forced into a lock-step, but the reader is always sure of the relative time-relationships.

Characterization

West's method of characterizing Tod Hackett is a subtle and in some ways a most deceptive exercise in establishing a "main" personage whose character is in many ways not the primary concern of the novel. It is probably too simple to adopt the widespread notion that Tod is intended merely as a reasonably "normal" young man who becomes involved with a set of Hollywood grotesques, and through whose eyes we see that involvement. West needed a character who could serve as an observer and an interpreter of the action. Tod serves better than any other single character to unify the action. Of all the characters in the novel, moreover, Tod is the least "flat." He has a wider variety of interests than does any other character in the novel, and these interests give extra dimensions and some malleability to his character. As an artist he sees people and events in terms of their potential for art, and this fact in itself lends Tod an objective capacity which most of the other characters lack. He is not, however, solely an observer of the action, as has so often been suggested. In spite of his objective capacity - almost but not quite the "negative capability" of the dedicated artist - he becomes involved in the crucial events of these people's lives. But he is not a voluntary participant. Though he prefers to resist involvement, he nonetheless becomes a participant, especially in the events of the life of Faye Greener. Through his involvement with her he becomes involved in the lives of other characters whose lives touch or parallel hers. Indeed, this involvement becomes in some ways an intimate one.

Character By Stereotype

In the opening section there is also a quick glimpse of West's method of encapsulating minor characters, frequently by means of a **cliche** or a set of cliches. In paragraphs three to five of chapter 1, the reader sees a little fat man dressed in cork helmet, polo shirt, and knickers. As a descent into the grotesque realities of the real and present world from the romance of the Napoleonic wars, this absurd figure screams authoritatively through a megaphone, directing the movie armies to a stage set. The little man is the most thoroughgoing stereotype of his kind that West could create, and the sheer triteness of the stereotype is the essence of the characterization. In the presentation of minor characters, this is one of West's most common devices of characterization, and one of his most effective.

In some ways the technique of character-creation by stereotype (Comerchero calls it by "**cliche**") is the prevalent method of characterization in *The Day of the Locust.* Throughout the first section, with the exception of Tod, the characters spring into fictional life as one stereotype or another - so much so, indeed, that each character takes on the quality of an abstraction or even the quality of a symbol. By means of several brief incidents Abe Kusich comes to life as the abstraction of a truculent dwarf who subsists by his wits on the edges of society - in this instance on the edge of Hollywood society. Claude Estee emerges as an abstraction of the kind of artist who is submerged entirely in his art, and his guests become a gallery of Hollywood stereotypes. Mrs. Jenning is less a person than a symbol of the "high class" call-house madam who "makes vice attractive by skillful packaging." In this section the characterization of Faye Greener is mostly indirect, serving as preparation for the direct characterization that becomes possible when we meet her for the first time in the second section of the novel.

Tod As "Reflector"

Though Tod appears to be the "central" character in *The Day of the Locust*, the novel does not seem to be "about" Tod. Of all the main personages in the novel, Tod suggests through his basic character much less than the other characters do about the Hollywood society which appears to be West's principal concern. As an integral part of the novel, Tod seems most important as an observing consciousness through whom the other characters are revealed and whose frequently non-participatory comments interpret the events. Tod seems most important as a "reflector" of people and events, rather than as a personage whose character is important in and for itself.

Themes

Of the ten major **themes** that help to inform *The Day of the Locust*, more than half appear in at least a beginning phase in the first section of the novel, and some of them appear in a fully developed state. Among the latter, the most obvious is the **theme** that nothing is what it seems to be. Tod's observations of the bizarre architectural styles and the camouflage of people's costumes establish this **theme** strongly. Furthermore, the **theme** that "few things are sadder than the truly monstrous" appears explicitly as West's statement at the end of chapter 1. The essential absurdity of man's pretensions to greatness and nobility appear full-blown in the absurd aspirations of Abe Kusich and Claude Estee, and it is suggested in the partial portrait of Harry Greener in the first section of the novel. The universal role of frustrated sex in the modern apocalypse is clearly suggested in Abe's grotesque introduction to Tod outside the doorway of a "slut," and in Tod's helpless fascination with

Faye Greener. The power of frustrated sex is suggested also - in preparation for fuller development later - in me early stages of Homer's consuming desire for Faye. Further, in the "fever eyes" and restless hands of Homer is an early suggestion of the **theme** that the people have never lived who have come here to die, and these are early suggestions also of the **theme** that these people have been cheated of their dreams. Most of these latter **themes** are merely introduced in the first section, as a prelude to full development in later sections.

Motifs

At least three obvious and ingenious motifs appear for the first time in the opening section of the novel. The first is the image of Tod's painting of "The Burning of Los Angeles," which reappears incrementally at crucial times throughout the novel. The second is the phrase "people who have come to California to die," which West uses almost as a composer would use a leitmotif in a musical composition. The third is the recurring reference to people in terms of performer and audience, as in "The Dancers" of Tod's painting, a group in which the performers change but in which the audience remains the same, full of passive expectation that drives the performers to greater and greater exertions all the time.

Symbols

In a literary work so densely symbolic in texture as *The Day of the Locust*, "symbol hunting" quickly becomes an activity of almost senseless supererogation. On the other hand, West frequently creates symbols of a special kind or quality, and the reader can gain special insights by giving these symbols special notice. As has already been mentioned in the section on characterization, West's methods of characterization tend to endow most of his characters with symbolic qualities. Perhaps the most obvious of these is Homer Simpson, whom West calls the "model" of the person who has come to California to die. The use of the term "model" appears to make it very nearly the same as "symbol," and people in the mass are also symbolized as "masqueraders." Moreover, places are often equally "symbolic" of something. The "San Berdoo," for instance, becomes a symbol of a cross-section of Hollywood society in the sense that it is a microcosm of that society, much as Claude Estee's mansion is a symbol of the effete world inhabited by "successful" Hollywood artists. In the first section of the novel there is also some more subtle and abstract symbolism. A good example of this kind of symbolism occurs in the opening phrase. The story begins "around quitting time," which is a phrase carrying far more than its literal, intrinsic meaning. In Tod's life, the whole novel takes place during a crucial phase that is in many ways a more comprehensive and final "quitting time," as the conclusion of the story makes quite clear.

Techniques

In perfecting his narrative technique, West learned to use a large number of special devices. Sometimes he used them singly, but more often he used them in combination with each other, and the disciplined use of these devices gives to West's prose its unique quality. One of the stylistic techniques peculiar to *The Day of the Locust* is West's deliberate manner of speaking of appearance as though it is actuality, as he does in the opening paragraphs of the novel. The device is actually a "reverse simile." That is, instead of saying that the people outside his window "look like" an army - which would have been the truth of the observation - he refers to them openly as an army, though it is an army in appearance only. As West continues to speak in this fashion, the reader learns only by obvious inference that the army merely resembles an army and is an illusion. Throughout *The Day of the Locust* this is one of West's most effective devices.

Early in the novel, West also makes effective use of the devices of **foreshadowing** and the plant. As foreshadowing, the scene at the beginning of the novel anticipates the crucial scenes on the movie lot in chapter 18, and the description of Tod's painting anticipates the real events at the end of the novel. As plants, the indirect remarks upon Faye Greener (including the speculation that she might be already one of Mrs. Jenning's girls) become crucial details by the end of the novel.

Throughout the novel, West makes regular and heavy use of the standard figures of speech, especially of **simile** and **metaphor**, frequently employing them both together in the same verbal unit. Though most prose writers are chary of complex figurative combinations of this kind, West uses them with rare discipline that gives his prose the compression of poetry without impairing the effect of the prose. In the first section (chapter 4), for instance, one finds this brilliant if brittle combination of **metaphor** and **simile** inside the same sentence: "Through a slit in the blue serge sky poked a grained moon that looked like an enormous bone button." In similar fashion, West uses his language to create a special kind of "double paradox" like that in which (chapter 1) the artificial effects of natural light look like artificial (neon) light that in turn makes the ugliness of nature appear "almost beautiful."

Special Effects

More than most modern novelists, West achieves in his prose a number of special effects, particularly in *The Day of the Locust*. The most obvious and pervasive of these effects is the persistence with which West views the world pictorially through the eyes of Tod, who has been trained as an artist. The effect - as Tod clearly indicates in his speculations upon the great painters whose art has most influenced his own attitudes - is sometimes as though the reader is seeing Tod's world in the form of a painting by Goya, Daumier, Picasso, Rosa, Guardi, Desiderio, or Janvier. A lesser but still important aspect of this pictorial approach is the extent to which so much is seen as though it is a movie script, with all its concrete research and its **cliches** of "movie talk." The specific details of costume in the second paragraph of the novel is an outgrowth of West's work as a script writer, as are the bizarre and deliberately irrelevant details of movie sets, the sheer triteness of Faye's aspirations to be a movie star, and the revealing **cliches** of the "movie talk" at Claude Estee's, especially in the pontifically repeated **cliche** "It's good, but it won't film" and its variations. Closely related to these special effects is the effect which West produces by deliberately writing in the hyperbole of moviedom. In describing the movie soldiers in the first paragraph, for instance, he evokes all the hyperbolic language of movie advertising by describing the sound of the horses as "the tattoo of a thousand hooves." The phrase sets the tone of these scenes, and it never quite dissipates throughout the novel.

SECTION 2: HOMER SIMPSON, CHAPTERS 7-12

In this section of the novel, the point of view is largely confined to the consciousness of Homer Simpson. The section begins with an explanation of why Homer left Iowa and came to Los Angeles. The section includes the Romola Martin "flashback" (chapter 8), a series of **episodes** devoted to revealing Homer's character (chapters 9–10), and the **episodes** in which he meets the Greeners and becomes infatuated with Faye (chapters 11–12).

Setting

Except for the interpolated scene which takes place in Wayneville, Iowa, the scenes in this section are set entirely at Homer's house and in the Greeners' apartment in the "San Berdoo."

Viewpoint

In much the same way as Tod's viewpoint dominates the first section of the novel, Homer's viewpoint dominates the second section. The viewpoint becomes less consistent in this section, however, with the pure omniscience of the author's persona breaking through and going beyond Homer's viewpoint. Logically these shifts are startling and sometimes confusing, especially to a sensitive reader.

Exposition

The integrated **exposition** in *The Day of the Locust* continues for an extraordinary distance into the novel, partly because the viewpoint is "shuffled" between Tod and Homer in the first two sections of the novel. Since the reader is not thoroughly introduced to Homer until the second section begins with chapter

8, there is little need until then for expository material dealing with Homer. Even then, having become partially acquainted with Homer in the latter part of the first section, the reader does not know exactly what kind of person he is or anything about his personal background until it becomes necessary to present his full character and personality and to give an essential **episode** from his past life in chapter 8 and in the chapters immediately following. The purpose of the Romola Martin **episode** is almost entirely expository, as are the subsequent small incidents that bit by bit establish the character of Homer, so that the crucial **episodes** of the main story-structure can unfold with adequate preparation. Beyond this section, however, the **exposition** is largely completed and therefore ceases as a special introductory technique.

Characterization

Unlike the characterization of Tod Hackett, which has some degree of "roundness" (See E. M. Forster's *Aspects of the Novel* for the classic description of "flatness" and "roundness" in fictional characterization), Homer Simpson is an excellent example of West's capacity to create complex but basically "flat" characters who are so thoroughly dominated by traumas and motivated by automatic, involuntary responses that they become symbolic abstractions of certain kinds of human characteristics. Homer, for instance, is a symbolic abstraction of almost completely repressed sexuality. Added to this, his twenty years of deadening labor as a bookkeeper make him also a symbolic abstraction of the "cheated ones" who have come to California to die. Homer's hands, which appear to have an independent life of their own, are a brilliant accessory to the characterization of Homer. A dramatic clue to Homer's many repressions, especially to his repressed sexuality, these hands - lying in a basin of cold water "like a pair of strange aquatic animals" - have sometimes been compared with Wing Biddlebaum's in the story "Hands" by Sherwood Anderson. Indeed, Homer's eerily independent hands are part of a motif in modern American fiction, including not only Wing Biddlebaum's hands but also those of Peter Boyle in *Miss Lonelyhearts* and those of Blind Pig in Nelson Algren's *The Man with the Golden Arm*.

The minimal characterization of Romola Martin has been created almost exclusively as a foil for the characterization of Homer Simpson. Without the Romola Martin **episode**, which has no particular function apart from Homer, one understands certain essential things about Homer that could not be revealed in any other way.

Themes

Most of the **themes** that first appear in section 1 are still developing in section 2, but in section 2 some of them reach their fullest development. With the full development of the character of Homer, for instance, comes also the full impact of the **theme** that the people who come to California to die have actually never lived at all. For the same reason, we sense in this section also the real if not quite the full significance of the **theme** that submerged violence lurks in suppressed sexual desires. One begins to recognize the latent violence in Homer's almost total sexual suppressions.

Motifs

Since motifs are by definition phenomena that recur throughout a work, most of the motifs that appear in section 1 reappear in succeeding sections of the novel. Most obvious in section 2 is the strong recurrence of the audience-performer motif in Harry's involuntary spasm of performance before the inert "watcher" Homer in chapter 11. Other motifs appear recognizably for the first time in section 2, however. Here Homer's hands become an actual motif of sexual repression, for instance; and with his impotence in the Romola Martin **episode** begins a motif of impotence that recurs with increasing frequency and variety of interpretation throughout the narrative. Though the motif of impotence begins here as purely sexual, it quickly becomes a motif of generalized impotence. Further, the **episode** of the lizard and the flies begins a motif on the oppressed versus the oppressors, with the sympathy, like Homer's, on the side of the oppressed (or as in the "victim's laugh" of Harry, the same motif could be called that of victims versus victimizers or even abstractly "murderees" versus "murderers"). The people symbolized by Homer are, of course, all "victims" or "murderees." With the beginning of the fatal illness of Harry Greener begins also a motif which shows modern human beings, like Faye and Harry, able to feel but not able to discriminate or to register and express real sorrow. All the "victims" in the book are so afflicted, as the motif repeatedly demonstrates.

Techniques

One of the first things the reader notices in section 2 is the specific, concrete, realistic description of the gross and tasteless architecture of Homer's house. For a writer who is considered a creator of the symbolic and the abstract, West is surprisingly good at using realistic and even naturalistic descriptive techniques. Moreover, as in the earlier section, West continues to rely heavily upon **imagery**. In particular, he frequently uses the **simile**, as in his comparing Homer with "one of Picasso's great sterile athletes," which also represents one of his pictorial effects (chapter 8). West continues also to pile up similes, as in the two successive short sentences (chapter 8) where he speaks of Homer's fingers twitching "as though troubled by dreams" and then of their twining together "like a tangle of thighs in miniature." The use of **foreshadowing** continues also, in a most crucial statement (chapter 12) that in the matter of lust Homer had escaped in the case of Romola Martin but that "he wouldn't escape again."

Special Effects

A most unusual special effect in section 2 is a variation upon the pictorial basis of the description, though this effect is perceived by Homer's consciousness instead of Tod's. In the grocery store (chapter 9) the natural colors of foods are enhanced by the colors shed by artificial lights.

SECTION 3: THE FUNERAL, CHAPTERS 13-17

This section of the novel contains the five chapters that deal principally with the illness and death of Harry Greener, along with all the other circumstances and developments that are connected with this major event in the novel. The section begins with Harry at home in bed after his attack of illness at Homer's house. The section includes also the "party" at Earle Shoop's camp in the canyon, the description of Harry's performances in the barrooms, the account of Harry's death along with Faye's decision to work for Mrs. Jenning, and the chapter on Harry's funeral.

Setting

This section contains a wide variety of specific settings. It opens in Harry's apartment in the "San Berdoo," switches to Earle

Shoop in front of Hodge's saddlery store, and switches again to Earle's camp in the canyon. The section then returns to a scene in Harry's bedroom, including as an interpolated section the account of Harry's habitual personal performances in public barrooms. The scene then explicitly opens in Harry's apartment for the scene wherein Tod finds Harry dead, and this section of the novel ends with the funeral scene at Holsepp's funeral parlor.

Viewpoint

At the beginning of this section the point of view apparently shifts from Homer's section back to Tod's point of view. But as a matter of fact the viewpoint does not remain with Tod in this section. Instead it fluctuates between Tod and Homer whenever the focus of the narrative appears to have one character or another as the center of consciousness. But there is no predictable pattern to these shifts, and the purely omniscient viewpoint continues to take over at random for short scenes or for short dissertations by West's authorial persona. This use of viewpoint continues to the end of the novel, and it is sometimes confusing. The apparent breakdown of any consistent management of point of view has caused several critics to argue that the viewpoint of the novel is weak and disturbing, adversely affecting the unity of the whole narrative.

Exposition

For all practical purposes, **exposition** as a special introductory device has ceased to operate by now, leaving only the use of **exposition** for whichever materials may require expository instead of narrative or descriptive treatment.

Characterization

Four characters are given their fullest characterization in this section, even though some of them have appeared in the narrative before this time. All of these personages are characterized, as Comerchero says, by **cliche**, so that they emerge as lively stereotypes. The most fully developed and the most complex of these characters is Faye Greener, who has been part of the story for a considerable time without ever emerging fully characterized. In this section, however, the reader begins to get some insight into her inner self. In a scene in her room (chapter 13) Tod discovers that "being with her was like being backstage during an amateurish, ridiculous play" and that as an actress she "had learned from bad models in a bad school." She aspires to all the Hollywood **cliches** of success, and yet, as a person, she is capable of becoming one of Mrs. Jenning's girls and at the same time of keeping Tod at a distance. As a person she appears to have no character except the character that her daydreams have given her. As for Harry, he emerges as a cheap but amazingly versatile vaudeville performer who has never had any identity save that of his own "skit characters," and even in vaudeville he has never been anything but a "fall guy" for other performers. The most shallow and two-dimensional of all the characters is Earle Shoop, who has all the superficial trademarks of the cowboy movie personality, though the trademarks are pasted on, as it were, so that he merely resembles a "mechanical drawing." Miguel, with his dark Armenian eyes, brown skin, and curly black hair, is a symbolic abstraction of male sexuality, which is the only role he has to fulfill in the narrative.

Themes

In the impossible aspirations of Faye and Harry Greener particularly there is in this section an intensification of the **theme** that human pretense to greatness and nobility is merely absurd. In this section there is also, in the small crowd of strangers who leave

Harry's funeral looking for greater excitement, a magnification of the **theme** that the "cheated ones" are individually passive but violent en masse. Further, the advancing development of Homer's preoccupation with Faye gives greater credence to the **theme** that the submerged violence of the people is always rooted in suppressed sex. In this section for the first time one begins to see, in Tod's growing awareness and in Homer's inability to adopt poses, the rise of the **theme** that an awareness of the meaninglessness of life is the result of a necessary state of self-consciousness. In this section one also sees for the first time how thoroughly life imitates art - in the extent to which the lives of Faye and Harry Greener are only extensions of the arts of vaudeville and the motion picture.

Motifs

In section 3 there is a recurrence of Tod's painting as a motif (chapter 13), and a new motif begins with the songs of the birds in chapter 14. Though this is rather late for the appearance of any motif that is intended to serve recurrently throughout the novel, West uses the motif of bird song repeatedly in chapter 14 as a tone and mood setter. This motif may actually have its beginning with the bird song at the end of chapter 12. At any rate, the motif of song serves as a build-up to the music that is played during the funeral. At this juncture in the narrative one remembers also that Faye had habitually antagonized her father by the singing of "Jeepers Creepers."

Symbols

Several symbols appear in section 3. Among them are the display window of the saddlery store (chapter 14), which emerges as a symbol of the real West that has become the movie West; the champion fighting cock that serves as a symbol of overt, aggressive male sexuality (chapter 14); the blood on the tips of the quail feather quills, which functions as a symbol of the flesh that weights or drags down the spirit (chapter 14); the dance between Faye and Miguel, which is rather obviously a symbolic ritual of the act of mating (chapter 14); and the public barrooms which for Harry are the counterparts if not actual symbols of the theater (chapter 15).

Techniques

Among the stylistic techniques that West uses in section 3, the most obvious and the most effective are the many similes. One can hardly help noticing the startling and appropriate references to Faye's "egglike self-sufficiency" and to Earle's "polelike appearance" (chapter 14). Nor can one avoid mention of the hummingbird and the bluejay, whose flight "burst the colored air into a thousand glittering particles like metal confetti" (chapter 14). As in the other sections, West also makes effective use of **foreshadowing** in the remark, during the dance, that Faye "seemed to know what he [Miguel] was thinking and to be thinking the same thing" (chapter 14). Moreover, at the end of chapter 14 Tod again adopts the role of Jeremiah and foretells the "civil war" among "America's madmen," and he asks himself whether all doomsayers are "such happy men."

SECTION 4: THE COCK FIGHT, CHAPTERS 18–23

This section contains two **episodes** important to the overall structure of the novel: Tod's tour of the movie studio (including the incident in which Mt. St. Jean collapses under the assault of the movie soldiers), and the cock fight in Homer's garage, which is a crucial scene in the lives of the major characters of the novel.

This section begins with Tod's tour of the "Waterloo" set (chapter 18) and goes on to the scene with the Loomises at Homer's house, when Tod decides to stop chasing Faye (chapter 19). Chapter 20 is the scene in which Tod, Homer, and Faye go to a night club; chapter 21 is the scene of the cock fight; and chapter 23 is the pivotal scene in which Abe Kusich engages in a free-for-all fight with Earle and Miguel in the living room of Homer's house.

Setting

The first setting in section 4 is the motion picture lot in which Tod wanders looking for Faye, and the second setting is the office where Tod finds Faye waiting for him (chapter 18). The setting then switches to Homer's house for the dinner with Faye, Homer, and Tod, including the backyard scene where the Loomises first appear (chapter 19). The next important setting is the night club where Faye and Homer take Tod (chapter 20). The setting then switches to the garage in Homer's house for the cock fight scene, and to Homer's living room for the fight involving Abe, Earle, and Miguel (chapters 21–22).

Viewpoint

In section 4 the point of view holds mostly to Tod as the center of consciousness of the narrative, but as in previous sections there are passages which make the reader wonder whether the viewpoint is not also Homer's or that of pure omniscience.

Characterization

The next-to-last section of a novel is not ordinarily early enough in a narrative to warrant the introduction of important new characters, but with the Loomises, West manages a tardy introduction and a legitimate one. They are merely generic characters whose purpose in the novel is to spark the apocalyptic violence which brings the novel to its conclusion. The fact that they are generic characters helps to justify their late introduction, and the same fact aids West in using to peak effectiveness his technique of characterization by stereotype. Adore is the classic stereotype of the precocious child entertainer, and Mrs. Loomis could be the model for the vapid housewife whose drive to bring fame to her offspring is instinctive, all-consuming, and fearful.

Themes

Though **themes** are no longer being initiated this late in the narrative, most of those originally established are being sustained. Most obvious in this section is the **theme** that life imitates art. At the end of chapter 20, West describes a man with eyes like those of a monk in paintings by Magnasco.

Symbols

In the passages devoted to Tod's tour of the movie studio, many things appear to take on symbolic overtones in the descriptions of various scenic locations. For example the scene in which the ancient god Eros (physical or "erotic" love) is discovered lying face down in a pile of trash seems to be a symbol of historic love descended into modern filth, and the "dream dump" itself is clearly symbolic of the indiscriminate dumping of all the most glorious aspects of the "American Dream," even though "no dream entirely disappears." The movie fiasco of Mont St. Jean is the symbolic counterpart of the historical fiasco. In much the same double-twist fashion, the young female impersonator at the bar is not so much a man pretending to be a woman as he is a man who is really a woman pretending to be a woman. This impersonator becomes a symbol of all women-men who pretend to be men-women. The disgusting scab-encrusted, meat-eating hen functions likewise as a sexual symbol. Though Earle and Miguel take meticulous care of the fighting cocks, they criminally neglect the hen, which serves as a symbol of the attitudes which such men have toward everything female in the world.

Themes

In the matter of technique, this is one of the most remarkable sections in the novel. In it, West uses most of the techniques that he has used elsewhere in the novel. Stylistically, the cock fight is a triumph of carefully detailed, starkly realistic narrative in the best manner of the naturalists of the 1930s. Yet West never relinquishes his capacity to use also a highly figurative style, with not only **metaphor** but hyperbolic **metaphor** like Mrs. Loomis's remark that California is "a paradise on earth," and with his usual scattering of **similes** like the description of Homer - "His servility was like that of a clumsy, cringing dog" - and like the widely quoted description of Faye's clingingly draped buttocks as "like a heart upside down."

Special Effects

This section is also rich in the peculiar kinds of special effects that West has created for this novel. The special pictorial effects, those of the famous painters and those of the movies, are actually combined here in order to show that the effects of the partly demolished movie sets are much the same as those achieved by certain painters "of Decay and Mystery," especially Rosa (chapter 18). Moreover, in the disastrous attempt to film the historical attack at Waterloo, West achieves a strangely inside-out view of history, as though history itself - which is as much the object of his **satire** as the moviemaking - is as senseless as the bungling of scene technicians. But in the same section of the novel he also achieves an almost Hemingwayesque effect in his spare, disciplined, compressed but colorful and dramatic account of the cock fight.

SECTION 5: THE CATASTROPHE, CHAPTERS 24-27

The concluding section of the novel contains only four chapters. These are the ones in which Tod visits Homer on the morning after the cock fight (chapter 24), in which Tod realizes what a dangerous emotional state Homer is in (chapter 25), in which Tod talks with the movie cowboys outside the saddlery store and then goes to a restaurant and visualizes the raping of Faye (chapter 26), and in which Homer is goaded into starting the riot of the crowd outside the movie theater (chapter 27).

Setting

The specific settings in this section are Homer's living room after Abe's fight with Earle and Miguel (chapters 24–25), the streets outside the saddlery store, and the dining room of a restaurant (chapter 26), and the streets and alleys outside a movie theater, where an enormous crowd gathers to see the stars at a movie premiere.

Characterization

As obviously planned from the beginning of the novel, this section provides the last bit of characterization necessary to achieve the full dimensions of Homer's character. Whatever he appears to be in the beginning, he is capable of the same vicious outburst of physical violence that is typical of the people who have been cheated of their dreams. In the last section of the novel we see the full emotional cycle which results in this kind of cataclysmic outburst.

Themes

All the major **themes** of the novel reach their fulfillment in this section. See the end of the section on motifs.

Motifs

Most of the main motifs have done their work by this stage of the novel, but in the last section there is an obvious recurrence of two motifs that had appeared earlier. Both have acquired meaning by virtue of all that has occurred between the last and the current reiteration of the motifs. In Tod's visualizing of the way things would go if he raped Faye in a vacant lot, he realized that even during such an act a bird would be singing somewhere close by; and near the end of the riot Tod's mind returns to the motif of his own painting, but he realizes that the subject of his art has now come to pass in actuality as he has tried to predict it in his art. The fulfillment of this motif has given peculiar force and meaning to the **theme** that life imitates art.

Symbols

The most obvious symbol in this section is Homer himself. As the living symbol of all the cheated ones, he actually motivates the cheated ones in an overt act of violence en masse, and he merges with the mass.

Techniques

In leading up to the cataclysm in this section, West provides a deluge of figurative language. At this important point in his narrative he is no longer satisfied with the usual form of the **metaphor** but he creates an impressive extended **metaphor** in which he speaks of the womb as "the perfect hotel" in which one has a "nine-months lease" (chapter 25). He speaks also of the foetal position which Homer assumes as the "original coil" of a spring released from its mechanical function. Moreover the section abounds in crisp and effective similes. Homer shakes his head slowly "like a dog with a foxtail in its ear" and sobs "like an ax chopping pine" while Tod's expression of sympathy is "like dynamite set off under a dam" (chapter 24). Ironically to Homer's naive understanding, he hears Faye in the bedroom moaning "like in pain," and he brings her some aspirin. In chapter 6 the waiter is referred to as "fly-like." There is also some strong foreshadowing in chapter 24, where Homer's attempt to talk out his confusion merely piles up the emotional pressure which he carries with him to the mob scene.

Special Effects

West achieves a peculiar special effect in the way in which Homer's attempt to describe the events of the previous night and morning results merely in a jumble of the usual time sequence (chapter 24). The most striking effect, however, is the noticeable result of careful polishing which West has lavished upon the climactic building of the riot scene which concludes the novel. The sureness of touch and the effective pacing of the scene is the obvious outcome of much reworking and meticulous polishing of the material.

THE DAY OF THE LOCUST

TEXTUAL ANALYSIS

THE CRITICS

Like the reaction of critics to all of West's novels, the initial response to *The Day of the Locust* was highly mixed and ultimately disappointing, as were the sales of the book. As the time approached for the novel to be published, West kept in touch with those reviewers whose initial responses could determine the commercial success of the novel. Because he was in California and had no way of knowing the immediate developments among members of the Eastern publishing establishment, he did everything he could to learn the reactions of reviewers to pre-publication copies of *The Day of the Locust*, and during the few weeks before the novel was to appear, West felt that he had reason to believe that reviewers would be encouraging. But as with most of his previous experiences with publishers and reviewers, some of the actual responses were confused, mixed, or otherwise disappointing, and some of the best ones appeared too late to have any material effect upon the reception of the book.

At first it appeared that such influential reviewers as Edmund Wilson, F. Scott Fitzgerald, George Milburn, Heywood Broun, Malcolm Cowley, Jack Conroy, and Erskine Caldwell could be relied upon to say good things about the novel. But even among these sympathetic critics there was an astonishing mixture of reaction, some of which disturbed West and perhaps adversely influenced sales of the novel. Milburn's essay, otherwise highly favorable, included a comment that the structure was choppy and episodic like that of a movie scenario. *The New Yorker* review, unexpectedly written by Clifton Fadiman instead of Robert Coates (who privately said that the novel was West's best one so far), openly branded the book surrealistic, though West insisted that he was not a surrealist author. Florence Haxton Britten's review in the *New York Herald Tribune* denied the surrealist label and called the book a superb piece of writing, but was unable to erase the effects of the *Fadiman* review. Other, more subtle comments by Edmund Wilson, Jack Conroy, and F. Scott Fitzgerald were published too late to be used in the advertising or to give the necessary boost to sales. Wilson's review in the New Republic was perceptive, appropriate, and almost entirely favorable, especially with regard to the author's use of his Hollywood materials. A substantial and complimentary review by Jack Conroy in Progressive Weekly appeared to have little effect. A highly satisfying private comment from F. Scott Fitzgerald was too late to be useful in the advertising. By far the most widely read comment appears to have been a Los Angeles Times review suggesting that the novel was mostly pornographic. As a result of this tissue of somewhat bizarre occurrences, and despite West's hope that sales would be respectable, the final sales records in February of 1940 showed that only 1,464 copies of *The Day of the Locust* had been sold. Indeed, West realized altogether a total of $1,280 from the four novels he had written.

These responses were typical of critical attitudes toward West during the thirties, when his novels were not part of the "graymash-potato" mainstream of social documentary novels and large-scale **realism** in prose fiction. Though a few writers and scholars continued to keep track of West's novels after his death in 1940, he was largely forgotten - or, more properly, continued to be neglected - until the *Complete Works of Nathanael West* was published in 1957. For reasons that are still not entirely clear, this event sparked an unprecedented interest in the writings of West, and with it came a surge of critical activity that is unique in the history of American letters in the twentieth century. The results of the whole sequence of events has been aptly described by Jonathan Raban in "A Surfeit of Commodities: The Novels of Nathanael West":

> **Like most mythical figures, his [West's] powers have been variously and exaggeratedly labelled: First American Surrealist, Sick Comedian, Dreamdumper, Nightmarist, Social Critic (of all things), Laughing Mortician. And for the mythmakers, West had an almost embarrassing abundance of convenient attributes; he was a Jew who renounced his religion; he was briefly expatriated during the twenties; he went the right distance out to the political left in the thirties; he worked in, and wrote about, Hollywood; he died young in a violent accident at the end of the decade. His four short, wildly uneven novels are a beachcomber's paradise; a junkshop of part-worn, part-used symbols and literary references. He is the indispensable minor modern novelist; once neglected, but now fully restored; use him anywhere, handy for your book or thesis. Especially suitable for Despair, Comedy, and Violence.**

In book-length studies, substantial scholarship did not begin until 1961, when James Light's *Nathanael West: An Interpretative Study* started a small landslide of book-length critiques of West. Light predicted a growing scholarly interest in the Westian universe, and within ten years at least five book-length studies of West followed upon Light's prediction. In 1962, Stanley Hyman wrote the University of Minnesota Series pamphlet study on West. He argues that *The Day of the Locust* lacks dramatic unity and therefore does not succeed as a novel, but he demonstrates that in general West "found objective correlatives for our sickness and fears." By 1964 there was another full-length study of West, this one by Victor Comerchero, with the subtitle of *The Ironic Prophet*. Contending that West's artistic method is rooted in the tensions between pathos and comedy, Comerchero says that *The Day of the Locust* represents a deepening of West's pessimism. "The novel is not a dramatized story," he says; "it is a prophecy" that gives us not a moral but a vision of holocaust. In 1967 Randall Reid produced *The Fiction of Nathanael West*. To him, *The Day of the Locust* is "a statement of what must follow the failure of the Christ Dream," and to him the apocalyptic conclusion of the novel is a fitting culmination of all that the previous novels had predicted for themselves. Not until 1970, however, did a really substantial full-length "standard" or "authorized" critical biography of West appear. This was Jay Martin's *Nathanael West: The Art of His Life*, a comprehensive biography that draws upon letters, private papers, memoirs, extensive interviews with friends and acquaintances of West, thorough discussions of his early years, and his involvement with social, political, and literary movements. Martin has plundered virtually all existing records of West's life, including newspaper materials and records from the motion picture studios. He provides a thorough and scholarly analysis of the conditions that influenced the writing and publication of *The Day of the Locust*. To Martin, *The Day of the Locust* is "both satiric and tragic," showing mankind at last preying on itself out of sheer perversion and boredom.

Since 1970 there have been other substantial attempts to analyze and interpret West, particularly Irving Malin's *Nathanael West's Novels* (1972), which performs the valuable service of giving us a close analysis and interpretation of the various possible meanings of West's novels. As indicated by the bibliography, since 1967 there has been a spate of periodical literature and sections in books, but much of this material deals with questions and problems already broached or adequately discussed in the various full-length studies on West.

THE DAY OF THE LOCUST

ESSAY QUESTIONS AND ANSWERS

....

Question: What is the significance of the ending of *The Day of the Locust*?

Answer: Critics have disagreed concerning the condition of Tod Hackett and the meaning of his imitating the siren at the end of the novel. Some critics have concluded that Tod has become insane, though it is much more likely that he has become, if anything, too sane as the result of his experience with the mob. He has become so sane that he sees for the first time, as nobody else can see, that the world has reached precisely the state of militant chaos that his own painting has predicted for it all along, and for precisely the same reasons. His imitation of the siren's wailing is the ultimate cry of the Jeremiah and of the Tiresias, the cry of the prophets whom he has represented as the observer of these events from their inception to their predictable conclusion. Tod's wail is a warning of the disintegration of the world. Otherwise this would not properly be an apocalyptic novel.

Question: Why is Homer referred to as resembling a poorly made automaton?

Answer: The image of Homer as an automaton is part of a whole complex of images in which West shows that human beings in the modern world are becoming more machines than human beings. To West, the modern world has subordinated all human needs - all human dreams and desires, all human aspirations, all human necessities - to a complex and unchecked machine age in which the differences between man and machine have become indistinguishable. In *The Day of the Locust*, Homer is a prime representative of the sometimes poorly articulated man-machine that has been created by the modern machine age.

    Moreover, Homer is characterized as less a real person than an intricate complex of programmed responses over which he had no control. Since West has created him to serve as the model for all the cheated people who have come to California to die, everything he is and does must be reconcilable with the last scenes of the novel, in which Homer has become almost literally an automaton, moving and acting awkwardly and without volition. It is ironic that even in terms of characterization Homer is not a well-integrated mechanical man. Yet if he were ever depicted as a well-integrated character he could not serve the purposes for which West had created him.

Question: Why does Harry Greener go into a frenzied vaudeville performance when he first meets Homer?

Answer: When Harry Greener first meets Homer Simpson, the old vaudeville performer is confronted with the one person in the novel who is the complete representative of all the inert, unresponsive, expectant "watchers" who are the counterparts of the "performers" in our society. This scene, then, is a crucial one in the whole actor-audience, performer-observer motif in the novel. According to West, all people fall into one of these two categories in our modern society, and each must live out his role in terms of the other - the audience-observers always expectant and demanding but inert and unresponsive, the actor-performers always called upon for greater and greater exertions of performance.

Therefore when Harry, the representative of the actor-performers, finds himself confronted by Homer, the very type of the inert observers, he is called upon to perform far past the limits of any human being's capacity. For this reason he becomes to all intents a mechanical man, wound up beyond the limits of the tension of his springs, and performing mechanically until his parts fly to pieces and he disintegrates.

Question: What is West's attitude toward history?

Answer: The only tangible clue to this answer is the **episode** in which Tod watches the movie soldiers in their assault upon Mont St. Jean. Here one sees that West preserves a peculiarly double-visioned view of history. Because West adopts his technique of speaking of the filming as though it is the real assault, one at first may be unsure whether he is making fun of the process of movie production or of real history. But upon close reading one perceives that he feels both history and the filming to be equally futile and ridiculous.

One who investigates the real historical assault soon realizes that the real tactical errors were just as ridiculous as those being made by the disorganized movie producers and directors. Indeed, in one place West only partly facetiously suggests that the movie people could change history if they wished, implying among other things that most people who see the movie will accept the movie version in place of the real events. It seems that West regards history as a series of random and futile events at best, from which the general public is not likely to learn much except through the capricious interpretations of the media of popular culture.

QUESTIONS FOR DISCUSSION AND RESEARCH

On "Black Humor" And The Comic Sense

1. What are the implications of the term "**black humor**"?

2. Why is *The Day of the Locust* sometimes regarded as an example of "**black humor**"?

3. How does "**black humor**" differ from other kinds of humor?

4. Is "**black humor**" regarded as a form of comedy? Why or why not?

5. West said that he considered himself a comic writer but not a humorist. What do you think he meant by making this distinction?

On The Comic Sense

1. Is there any valid comparison between *The Day of the Locust* and Ken Kesey's One Flew Over the Cuckoo's Nest? If so, what is the comparison?

2. Do Nathanael West and Richard Brautigan (*Trout Fishing in America*) appear to have any attitudes in common?

3. Does anything in *The Day of the Locust* evoke laughter?

4. In what ways is West's comic sense a serious commentary upon contemporary society?

On The Hollywood Novel

1. To what extent is *The Day of the Locust* a novel about the film industry?

2. Most of the characters in *The Day of the Locust* are "fringe people of the movie industry. What are the implications of this term?

3. Is the Hollywood of West's novel really any different from any other American suburban town of similar size? Explain.

4. Why is Hollywood an effective setting for a novel that deals with the "cheated people" in our society?

On Characterization In "The Day Of The Locust"

1. Is the characterization of Tod Hackett different from that of other characters in the novel? How, or why not?

2. What does Comerchero mean by the term "characterization by **cliche**" with regard to the characterization in *The Day of the Locust*?

3. In what ways is Homer a "model" of the people who have come to California to die?

4. Has Harry Greener lost the capacity to experience sorrow? Explain.

5. In what ways is Faye Greener a model for the modern sex symbol?

On West's Techniques

1. What are the differences, if any, between "techniques" and "special effects" in *The Day of the Locust*?

2. What does West gain by his heavy use of **similes** in the latter part of *The Day of the Locust*?

3. In what ways does West foreshadow coming events in *The Day of the Locust*?

4. To what extent does *The Day of the Locust* utilize the techniques of the movie script?

5. To what extent do the main characters in *The Day of the Locust* function as symbols of something besides themselves?

6. To what extent is Tod Hackett the "center of consciousness" in *The Day of the Locust*?

7. What did West mean when he referred to "my kind of joking"?

BRIGHT NOTES STUDY GUIDE

General Questions

1. What is meant by the term "authorial persona," and how does the "authorial persona" function in *The Day of the Locust*?

2. Is Tod Hackett the "hero" of *The Day of the Locust*? Explain.

3. Thackeray calls *Vanity Fair* "a novel without a hero." Is *The Day of the Locust* also a novel without a hero, and does it lack a hero in the same sense that *Vanity Fair* lacks a hero?

4. Is the San Bernardino apartment building a "microcosm" in the same sense that the Pequod is a microcosm in *Moby Dick*, or is it more like the asylum in *One Flew Over the Cuckoo's Nest*?

5. The description of the cock fight has been said to vaguely resemble Hemingway's literary style. To what extent is this assumption defensible?

6. Is Homer Simpson a modern Hamlet? Explain.

7. In what ways is the title *The Day of the Locust* appropriate to the story West tells?

8. How does West illustrate the **theme** that life imitates art?

9. Is West's "wasteland" the same kind of wasteland that T. S. Eliot depicts in his poem "The Waste Land"?

10. In Eliot's poem "The Waste Land" the poet suggests a solution to the conditions depicted in the poem. Does West offer a solution? If so, what is the solution? If not, why does he avoid suggesting a solution?

11. Is *The Day of the Locust* a surrealistic novel? Discuss.

TOPICS FOR PAPERS

On "Black Humor" And The Comic Sense

1. Major examples of "**Black Humor**" in *The Day of the Locust*.

2. A Study of Serious Comedy in *The Day of the Locust*.

3. The Humor of *The Day of the Locust* as a Typical Example of Contemporary American Humor.

4. The "**Black Humor**" of *The Day of the Locust* as a Special Commentary upon the Human Condition.

5. Is **Satire** a Legitimate Form of Comedy? Why or Why Not?

6. The Comic Sense and Absurdity in *The Day of the Locust*.

7. Objects of West's **Satire** in *The Day of the Locust*.

On The Comic Sense

1. A Comparison of the Comic Sense in *The Day of the Locust* and in Joseph Heller's *Catch-22*.

2. *The Day of the Locust* and Evelyn Waugh's *The Loved One*: A Comparison of the Comic Attitudes of the Two Authors.

3. The Influence of Great Painters upon the Comic Sense of West in *The Day of the Locust*.

4. The Development of West's Comic Sense from His Earliest Novels to *The Day of the Locust*.

On The Hollywood Novel

1. *The Day of the Locust* and Waugh's *The Loved One* as" Hollywood Novels."

2. Is *The Day of the Locust* a "Hollywood Novel" in the Same Sense that Budd Schulberg's *What Makes Sammy Run?* is a "Hollywood Novel"? Answer the question in a short comparative paper.

3. The Influence of the Movie Industry upon the Lives of the Characters in *The Day of the Locust*.

4. A Comparison of West's Description of Hollywood with Huxley's Description of Los Angeles in *After Many a Summer Dies the Swan*.

5. The "Hollywood Dream" as the "American Dream" Taken to Its Logical Conclusions.

On West's Techniques

1. Special Characteristics of West's Figurative Language in *The Day of the Locust*: The Use of **Similes** and Metaphors.

2. The Hollywood of *The Day of the Locust* and the Asylum of Kesey's *One Flew Over the Cuckoo's Nest*: A Comparison of Literary Techniques.

3. The Special Plot Structure of the Short Novel as Demonstrated by the Plot Structure of *The Day of the Locust*.

4. A Contrast Between the Basic Structure of Heller's *Catch-22* and West's *The Day of the Locust*.

5. The Influences of West's Experiences as a Hotel Employee upon His Techniques in Writing *The Day of the Locust*.

6. The Differences Between the Techniques of the Comic Strip as the Basis of *Miss Lonelyhearts* and the Techniques of the Movie Script as the Basis of *The Day of the Locust*.

General Suggestions For Paper Topics

1. Homer Simpson's Hands Compared with Those of Peter Doyle in *Miss Lonelyhearts*, Those of Wing Biddlebaum in Sherwood Anderson's "Hands," and Those of Blind Pig in Nelson Algren's *The Man with the Golden Arm*.

2. The Influences of Natural Phenomena Versus the Influences of Man-Made Phenomena upon the Lives of the People in *The Day of the Locust*.

3. The Motif of the Oppressed Versus the Oppressors (of the "Murderees" Versus the "Murderers") in *The Day of the Locust*.

4. Faye Greener as a Symbolic Abstraction of the "Love Goddess" in Popular Culture.

5. The "Omniscient Narrator" Compared with the Roles of Various "Third Person Reflectors" of the Authorial Persona in *The Day of the Locust*.

6. Tod Hackett as a "Jeremiah."

7. *The Day of the Locust* as a Novel that Conforms with Poe's Definition of a Short Poem.

8. A Comparison of the Short-Novel Structure of *The Day of the Locust* and the Long-Novel Structure of Heller's *Catch-22*.

9. A Comparison of the "Upside-Down-Inside-Out" World of Algren's *A Walk on the Wild Side* and the World of *The Day of the Locust*.

10. The Nature of the Comedy in *The Day of the Locust* and in Algren's *A Walk on the Wild Side*: A Comparison and Contrast.

11. The Characters in *The Day of the Locust* as Symbolic Abstractions.

12. Figurative Language as an Essential Quality of West's Literary Style in *The Day of the Locust*.

13. A Comparison of the Plot Structure of *The Day of the Locust* with the Structure of Two Other Short Novels of a Similar Length. (Suggested stories: Crane: *Maggie*; *A Girl of the Streets* or *The Blue Hotel*; Kafka: *The Metamorphosis*; Sartre: *Nausea*; Dostoevsky: *The Gambler*; Gogol: *The Overcoat*; Conrad: *Heart of Darkness* or *The Shadow-Line*.)

14. Is Tod Hackett Merely an Observer and not a Participator in the Events of *The Day of the Locust*?

15. Homer Simpson as a Fictional Character Who Represents One of the Essential Conditions of Modern Man.

16. The Possible Influences of Sartre's *Nausea* upon West's Conception of *The Day of the Locust*.

17. *The Day of the Locust* and the French Existentialists: A Study in Literary Influence.

BIBLIOGRAPHY

EDITIONS OF "THE DAY OF THE LOCUST" (EXCLUDING FOREIGN TRANSLATIONS)

The Day of the Locust. New York: Random House, 1939. Hardcover.

The Day of the Locust. London: Grey Walls Press, 1951. First British Edition.

The Day of the Locust. Introduction by Richard B. Gehman. New York: Bantam, 1953. Paperback.

The Complete Works of Nathanael West. Introduction by Alan Ross. New York: Farrar, Straus and Cudahy, 1957. Hardcover.

The Day of the Locust, The Dream Life of Balso Snell. Harmondsworth, Middlesex: Penguin Books, in Association with Secker and Warburg, 1957. Paperback. Not for sale in U.S.A. or Canada.

Miss Lonelyhearts and The Day of the Locust. New Directions, New Classics Series, 1962. Paperback.

The Day of the Locust. With a New Introduction by Budd Schulberg. New York: Time, Inc.; Time Reading Program, 1965. Paperback.

BOOKS ABOUT WEST

(For annotations, see section on *Day of the Locust* and the critics) Comerchero, Victor. *Nathanael West: The Ironic Prophet*. Syracuse: Syracuse University Press, 1964.

Cramer, Carter M. *The World of Nathanael West: A Critical Interpretation*. Emporia State Research Studies, vol. XIX, No. 4. Emporia, Kansas: Kansas State Teachers College, 1971.

Hyman, Stanley E. *Nathanael West*. University of Minnesota Pamphlets on American Writers, no. 21. Minneapolis: University of Minneapolis Press, 1962.

Light, James F. *Nathanael West: An Interpretative Study*. Evanston: Northwestern University Press, 1961.

Malin, Irving. *Nathanael West's Novels*. Carbondale: Southern Illinois University Press, 1972.

Martin, Jay, ed. *Nathanael West, A Collection of Critical Essays*. Twentieth Century Views. Englewood Cliffs, N. J.: Prentice Hall, Inc., 1971.

Martin, Jay. *Nathanael West: The Art of His Life*. New York: Farrar, Straus and Giroux, 1970.

Reid, Randall. *The Fiction of Nathanael West: No Redeemer, No Promised Land*. Chicago: University of Chicago Press, 1967.

White, William. *Nathanael West: A Comprehensive Bibliography*. Serif Series, Bibliographies and Checklists, no. 32. Kent, Ohio: Kent State University Press, 1975.

SECTIONS AND CHAPTERS IN BOOKS

Allen, Walter. "The Thirties: America." In *The Modern Novel in Britain and the United States*; pp. 167–172. New York: E. P. Dutton, 1964. For West, the comic sense is the only answer to the intolerable nature of the human condition in the modern world.

Auden, W. H. "Interlude: West's Disease." In *The Dyer's Hand and Other Essays*; pp. 238–245. New York: Random House, 1962. Calls West's books parables or cautionary tales.

Cowley, Malcolm. Exile's Return. New York: Viking Press, 1973. In a footnote to this book, originally written in 1934, Cowley calls *The Day of the Locust* "the best of the Hollywood novels."

Fiedler, Leslie. *Love and Death in the American Novel*; pp. 316–318, 461–467. New York: Criterion Books, 1960. Analyzes West in the light of Freudian psychology.

Gehman, Richard B. Introduction to *The Day of the Locust*. New York: New Directions Books, 1950.

Kernan, Alvin B. "The Mob Tendency: *The Day of the Locust*. "In The Plot of **Satire**. New Haven: Yale University Press, 1965. Traces the classic pattern of **satire** in the mob tendency of *The Day of the Locust*.

Podhoretz, Norman. "Nathanael West: A Particular Kind of Joking. " In *Doings and Undoings: The Fifties and After in American Writing*, pp. 66–75. New York: Farrar, Straus and Giroux, 1964. Explains West's "particular kind of joking" as an attitude in which human efforts to contend with the universe result only in absurdity.

Raban, Jonathan. "A Surfeit of Commodities: The Novels of Nathanael West. "In *The American Novel and the Nineteen Twenties*; edited by Malcolm

Bradbury and David Palmer, pp. 215–231. Stratforduponon-Avon Studies 13. London: Edward Arnold; New York: Crane, Russak, 1971. Raban classifies West's novels as "comic apocalyptic novels" and argues that West is basically a comic novelist. He describes West as a "marginal man" who could exist inside his work and outside it at the same time.

Wilson, Edmund. "The Boys in the Back Room." In *Classics and Commercials*. New York: Vintage Books, 1962. *The Day of the Locust* "has caught the emptiness of Hollywood" and West is "the first writer to make this emptiness horrible."

ARTICLES ABOUT "THE DAY OF THE LOCUST" IN PERIODICALS

Aaron, Daniel. "Writing for Apocalypse." *Hudson Review 3* (Winter 1951): 634–36. Suggests that in *The Day of the Locust* West has used Hollywood as the perfectly appropriate locale and environment for the American apocalyptic novel - "America carried to its logical conclusions."

Coates, Robert M. "The Four Novels of Nathanael West, That Fierce, Humane Moralist." *Review in the New York Herald Tribune*, 9 May 1957. Insists that West is not only an Old Testament moralist but a humane one.

Collins, Carvel. "Nathanael West's *The Day of the Locust* and Sanctuary." *Faulkner Studies* 2, no. 2 (Summer 1953): 23–24. An impressive series of parallels between these two novels, showing that West has taken for his own a good deal of Faulkner's characterization.

Galloway, David D. "Nathanael West's Dream Dump." *Critique* 6, no. 3 (Winter 1963–64): 46–64. Shows that Hollywood was an especially appropriate locale for West's purposes in *The Day of the Locust*, since it could be both symbolic and microcosmic.

Gehman, Richard B. "Nathanael West: A Novelist Apart. " *Atlantic* 86 (September 1950): 69-72. Hollywood is a microcosm of "everything that is wrong with life in the United States."

Gilmore, Thomas B., Jr. "The Dark of the Cave: A Rejoinder to Kernan on *The Day of the Locust*." **Satire** *Newsletter* 2 (Spring 1965): 95-100. Argues that *The Day of the Locust* cannot legitimately be regarded as a satire.

Lokke, V. L. "A Side Glance of Medusa: Hollywood, the Literature Boys, and Nathanael West." *Southwest Review* 46, no. 1 (Winter 1961): 35-45. Argues that the main thesis of *The Day of the Locust*, as with all of West's novels, is that human needs are dependent upon the processes of an ever-expanding machine age.

Phillips, Robert S. "Fitzgerald and *The Day of the Locust*."*Fitzgerald Newsletter*, no. 15 (Fall 1961): 2-3. Shows a surprisingly large number of parallels between *The Day of the Locust* and *Tender Is the Night*, though some of the parallels are quite generalized.

Widmer, Kingsley. "The Hollywood Image." *Coastlines* 5, no. 1 (Autumn 1961): 17-27. Compares West with Schulberg, Mailer, and Fitzgerald as Hollywood novelists.

Williams, William Carlos. *The Day of the Locust. A review. Tomorrow*, 10 (November 1950): 58-59. Using *The Day of the Locust* as a gauge of West's developing talents, Williams argues that West might have become "the finest prose talent of our age."

www.ingramcontent.com/pod-product-compliance
Lightning Source LLC
LaVergne TN
LVHW011717060526
838200LV00051B/2930

*9 7 8 1 6 4 5 4 2 3 4 6 1 *